Statistical Analysis Simplified

Statistical Analysis Simplified

The Easy-to-Understand Guide to SPC and Data Analysis

H. James Harrington

Glen D. Hoffherr

Robert P. Reid, Jr.

McGraw-Hill

New York   San Francisco   Washington, D.C.   Auckland   Bogotá
Caracas   Lisbon   London   Madrid   Mexico City   Milan
Montreal   New Delhi   San Juan   Singapore
Sydney   Tokyo   Toronto

McGraw-Hill

A Division of The **McGraw·Hill** *Companies*

1 2 3 4 5 6 7 8 9 0 DOC/DOC 9 0 1 0 9 8 7

ISBN: 0-07-913729-6

Library of Congress Cataloging-in-Publication Data

Harrington, H.J. (H. James)
    Statistical analysis simplified : the easy-to-understand guide to SPC and
data analysis / H. James Harrington, Glen D. Hoffherr, Robert P.
Reid, Jr.
      p.   cm.
    Includes bibliographical references (p.   –) and index.
    ISBN 0-07-913729-6
    1. Process control—Statistical methods.   I. Hoffherr, Glen D.
II. Reid, Robert (Robert P.), Jr.   III. Title.
TS156.8.H36   1997
658.5—DC21
                                                97-38124
                                                   CIP

The sponsoring editor for this book was Patrick Muller. The editing supervisor was John M. Morris, and the production supervisor was Suzanne W. B. Rapcavage. Production was managed by John Woods, CWL Publishing Enterprises, Madison, WI. It was designed and composed at Impressions Book and Journal Services, Inc., Madison, WI.

Contents

About the Series

Statistical Analysis Simplified is one title in McGraw-Hill's Harrington's Performance Improvement Series. The series is designed to meet an organization's need to understand the most useful approaches now available to bring about improvements in organizational performance as measured by:

► Return on investment,
► Value added per employee, and
► Customer satisfaction.

Each title in the series is written in an easy-to-read, user-friendly style to reach employees at all levels of an organization. Our goal is to present complex methodologies in a way that is simple but not simplistic. The following are other subjects covered in the books in this series:

► Statistical Process Control
► Process Redesign
► Process Reengineering
► Establishing a Balanced Scorecard
► Reliability Analysis
► Fostering Teamwork
► Simulation Modeling
► Rewards and Recognition
► Managing the Change Process

We believe that the books in this series will provide an effective way to learn about these practices as well as a training tool for use in any type of organization. In each title in the series, the design features a series of icons in the margins that call your attention to different points. Use these icons to guide your reading and study:

Requirement, Rule,
or Principle

 Example

 Concept or Idea

 Quote

"Speak now
or forever hold your
peace."
—Everyman

 Guide

 Exercise

Dd Definition

This is a sample of
the text for the defi-
nition, or these are
more synonyms and
usages that are com-
monly found in the
English language.

 Checks and Alarms

You can improve
your creativity
by learning
about and using
tools that help
you see and
understand the
world from new
perspectives.
Discussion

It is our hope that you will find this series of Performance Improvement Management books enjoyable and useful.

H. James Harrington
Principal, Ernst & Young LLP
International Quality Advisor

About the Authors

Dr. H. James Harrington is one of the world's quality system gurus with more than 45 years of experience. He has been involved in developing quality management systems in Europe, South America, North America, and Asia. He currently serves as a Principal with Ernst & Young, LLP and is their International Quality Advisor. He is also chairman of Emergence Technology Ltd., a high tech software and hardware manufacturer and developer.

Before joining Ernst & Young LLP, he was president of the consulting firm Harrington, Hurd, and Rieker. He was a Senior Engineer and Project Manager for IBM, and for almost 40 years, he worked in quality function. He was chairman and president of the prestigious International Academy for Quality and the American Society for Quality Control. He has released a series of videos and CD ROM programs that covered ISO 9000 and QS-9000. He has also authored a computer program on benchmarking, plus members' video tapes on performance improvement. He has written ten books on performance improvement and hundreds of technical reports.

The Harrington/Ishikawa Medal was named after him in recognition of his support to developing nations in implementing quality systems. China named him their Honorary Quality Advisor, and he was elected into the Singapore Productivity Hall of Fame. He has been elected honorary member of seven quality professional societies, and has received numerous awards and medals for his work in the quality field, including the 1996 Lancaster Award from ASQC in recognition of his work to further the Quality Movement internationally.

Glen D. Hoffherr is a senior consultant for James Martin Government Consulting. He has spent over 20 years in management in the high technology industry. For the last eight years he has been a consultant and author focusing on strategic planning, organizational design, change management, and creative decision making.

He has authored, co-authored, or been a contributing author to more than 15 books and numerous magazine articles. He is an animated, interesting, and entertaining speaker who has lectured at national and international conferences on five continents, and at numerous colleges and universities around the world.

He has worked with organizations in many fields including local, state, and national government, foreign governments, telecommunications, high technology, service, manufacturing, health care, and software.

Robert P. Reid, Jr., is a dynamic and innovative presenter, with over 30 years experience as an educator, author, speaker and organizational developer. Reid has written extensively in the areas of organizational change management, creative thinking, and systems design. He has worked with more than one hundred major organizations on six continents, and has conducted courses and seminars at seventeen universities. His ability to communicate complex systems issues in a clear non-threatening fashion is recognized world-wide.

Dedication

This book is dedicated to the two men who taught me the power of numbers. The first was my father, Robert P. Reid, Sr., who from an early age provided me with an endless set of mathematical games, puzzles, and conundrums that stimulated my ability to think quantitatively. The second was W. Edwards Deming, who taught me that most things in life cannot be measured. He was fond of saying, "The important things in life are unknown and unknowable. How can you measure the impact of an unhappy customer; for that matter how can you measure the impact of a happy customer?"

Bob Reid

Foreword

Why Numbers Are Important

Measurement stands as one of the great inventions of all time. Every day we make thousands of decisions—what to eat for breakfast, which route to take to work, and so forth. This book is about making better decisions using numbers. Many of our everyday decisions contain the question "How much?" or "How many?" The answers to these and many other questions involve measurement and numbers. "What time do I have to get up tomorrow?" The answer is a number, 6:30 A.M.

That answer is a measure of time. When ancient people first began measuring time, they based their measurements on observations of night and day, changing seasons, and cycles of the moon. These observations became the basis for units of measure that we now call days, months, and years. As life became more complicated, the Babylonians used the sundial to segment the day into 12 parts, each called an hour.

Measures of weight likewise go back to ancient times—over 5,000 years. Egyptian tombs dating to 4000 B.C. contain stone weights. Ancient Egyptians used weights on balance pans to weigh gold. And when you buy groceries, you base many of your purchasing decisions on this common measuring concept. If you ask yourself, "How much hamburger do I need to make meatloaf for my family?" the answer will be in pounds or kilograms. Think of your supermarket and the many everyday products that are bought and sold on the basis of weight. You can buy fresh meat, vegetables, butter, sugar, flour, and coffee by the pound or the kilogram. Many manufacturing processes are also controlled on the basis of weight. Chemical manufacturers measure the ingredients in their processes to ensure the quality of their products.

The history of measurement is a fascinating story of methods that evolved as civilization progressed. In ancient Egypt, the Nile flowed quietly for most of the year. Farmers tended their crops and worked their farms. When the spring floods roared down the Nile, all signs of their fields were washed away. After the flooding river deposited thousands of tons of rich silt on top of the fields, each farmer asked, "Where is my field?" Posts and stone markers could not withstand the flood waters. The solution the Egyptians developed was a means of measuring accurately from a distant point of reference beyond the flood waters. They invented surveying.

If you stop in a fabric store to buy cloth for a new garment, you ask yourself, "How long a piece of fabric do I need?" Length is another measuring concept that dates back over 5,000 years. Measuring length requires comparing one thing to another. Measurement sticks were used to determine length in ancient times. Because sticks could get lost and were of different sizes, it became more convenient to use parts of the human body as standards for length measurement. When building the pyramids, the Egyptians used a measure of length called a *cubit,* which was the distance from a man's forearm to his fingertip. Body standards were so practical that other parts of the body became standards of measurement. The Romans used the width of the thumb and called it an *uncia,* forerunner of the English word *inch.* A man's foot was approximately 12 thumbs long; thus 12 inches became a foot. This system worked well until the Middle Ages and the spread of commerce. Because a tradesman could go broke if he had large hands and feet, a universal standard was needed. But whose foot would become the standard? The answer was "the king's." To this day, we do not say, "Pass me the king's foot" when we want to measure something. We say, "Pass me the ruler."

The numbers used to express measurement also evolved over time. Although base ten numbers seem very logical and familiar to us, it took centuries for the base ten system to evolve. The ancient Egyptians, Babylonians, Greeks, and Romans used symbols different from those in our current system. Imagine a very early counting system in which a sheepherder made a mark on a stick or piece of bark for each sheep he owned: A large herd would require a lot of bark and a great many marks. A shorthand developed to represent a group of sheep with a special mark. These special marks, like spoken and written language, evolved differently in different societies (see examples).

Numerals for 1, 10, 100 from Five Civilizations

Egyptian 3000 **B.C.**

) 1	∩ 10	৯ 100

Babylonian 1500 **B.C.**

V 1	⟨ 10	V⟩ 100

Chinese 500 **B.C.**

— 1	+ 10	百 100

Greek 400 **B.C.**

α 1	ι 10	ρ 100

Roman 200 **B.C.**

I 1	X 10	C 100

Arabic **A.D.** 800

1	10	100

Not only did symbols differ, but methods for calculations and arithmetic took many forms. About A.D. 600, the Hindus made one of the greatest mathematical breakthroughs of all time with the concept of zero. They invented the symbol *0,* meaning empty space. Modern numerals use zeros as place holders—for instance, 307 is short for three of hundreds, none of tens, and seven of ones. The concept is so simple but so very powerful.

The Power of Numbers

The power of numbers lies in simplicity, but simplicity can be misleading. Oliver Wendell Holmes said, "I would not give a penny for simplicity on this side of complexity, but I would give my purse for simplicity on the other side of complexity." Numbers are powerful tools for making better decisions, but numbers alone cannot make decisions. People make decisions.

People run processes. People manage organizations. People create the future. Ultimately, there are no answers, only more questions. We designed this book to help you think about ways to use numbers to make better decisions. You must make the decisions. Numbers help you answer the three basic questions concerning every decision:

1. Am I getting the results I want?
2. Is there too much variation in the results I get?
3. Are the results I get stable over time?

Let's try out these questions on chocolate chip cookies. The first question is

1. Am I getting the results I want? Are the cookies
   — the right size?
   — done correctly?
   — the proper thickness?

To determine the answers, you must have a standard or reference. Here is our standard: We like our cookies 2 inches in diameter, dark brown on the edges, soft, and with lots of chocolate chips. If the cookies meet these requirements, then by our standards they are good.

The second question is

2. Is there too much variation between cookies? Are the cookies
   — the same size?
   — made with the same number of chocolate chips?

To answer these questions, you must compare each cookie to the others.

The third question is

3. Are they stable over time? Will each batch of cookies
   — produce the same results?
   — be baked the same way every day?
   Have I found a way to make good cookies consistently?

You may not care about baking cookies, but the least threatening way to talk about measurement is to use simple examples. Baking a pie, driving a car across a bridge, and correcting your golf swing are examples of actions that can help you visualize how numbers and measurement can help you understand the issues you face.

As you read this book, try to translate the logic and power of measurement to your own applications. Measurement can be fun if you overcome your fear of math. The good news is that because you live in the computer age, you probably will never have to use the boring long division you learned in school. Measurements and numbers pour out of computers. We are tapping more of their potential every day. This is not a book about computers. It is not even a book about mathematical calculations. It is a book about how you can use measurement, numbers, and data to help you do what you have to do and make better decisions. If you don't know what you want to do, then this book cannot help you.

Each of the book's 10 chapters can stand by itself. However, we have structured the book so that each chapter builds on what you have learned in the preceding one. Following are the concepts covered in each chapter.

CHAPTER 1. How to use measurement as an objective language for promoting honest and open communication

CHAPTER 2. How looking at groups of numbers gives you insights into the way things are

CHAPTER 3. How you can find one number that represents a large group of numbers

CHAPTER 4. How looking at sets of numbers over time reveals trends and movement

CHAPTER 5. How to use data as a guideline for deciding when to take action for change and when to leave things alone

CHAPTER 6. How to use numbers to compare what you are doing with what your customers and end users want

CHAPTER 7. How to experiment to find and identify better methods

CHAPTER 8. How to divide things into subsets so you can study your process

CHAPTER 9. How to find out why things are as they are by identifying cause-and-effect relationships

CHAPTER 10. How to put all these good ideas to work in your organization

Following the 10 chapters are two appendices. **Appendix A** provides additional information about control charts, and **Appendix B** gives answers to questions and quizzes found throughout the book. We have included a bibliography of resources that will give you additional information about the use of numbers and a glossary of terms used throughout the book.

The CD/ROM inside the back cover provides a visual introduction to the power of measurement. The chapters in this book are like tools in a toolbox. They won't do you much good if they stay in the box. For a hammer to work, you must pick it up and use it. Rarely do you use every tool in your toolbox for a given job. On some jobs, certain tools may get used more than once. When you first begin using tools, you may not be very handy with some of the them. Don't become discouraged. Keep using the tools, and you will become more adept at making them work for you. We urge you to try one or two of these tools the next time you need to make a decision. As you become proficient with one tool, begin using another to make your job easier. If a tool complicates your decision-making process, don't use it. We know that once you start using these tools well, you will use them often.

1

Measurement

An Objective Language for Communication

Introduction

This chapter will give you practical insight into the nature of measurement. Measurements have different uses in the management of an organization's work. The first section of the chapter explains that measurement can be used to set directions, establish plans, or track work. All three are important; all must be done. The second section tells you to get MAD—measure, analyze, and do. These elements are the big three of every individual and organizational decision. The third section introduces the measurement chain. Measurement in itself does not accomplish much. Measurement must be connected to key success factors. Numbers, like people, assume different sizes and shapes. Matching the type of measurement with the type of decision to be made is important. The favorite question of every four-year-old—"Why?"—applies to measurement as well. Answering the question of why numbers are important to you is your first step on the road to making decisions based on sound numerical information. The chapter ends with simple step-by-step guidelines for collecting numbers by using a check sheet.

Three Points of View

The greatest obstacle to the use of numbers is the mistaken idea that they are difficult to understand. Now, we'll admit that using numbers to make better decisions can involve some high-powered mathematics, but you don't have to be a mathematician to use numbers.

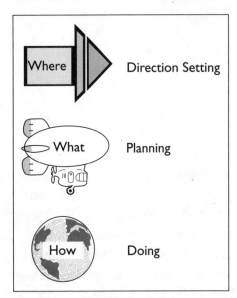

You can view everything you do from three important points of view. The first is setting the *direction* you want to move in. The second is *planning* how you are going to move in that direction. The third is actually *doing* the work to get to where you want to go—implementing your plans. For an organization to succeed, everyone, every day must consider and take account of these three points of view.

In many organizations, the executives alone set direction. Managers do the planning work as part of their back-office responsibilities. The rest of the employees implement the tasks on the front line. All projects involve setting direction, planning how to move in that direction, and implementing the plans.

We have all planned, cooked, or enjoyed meals. Someone must set the direction and determine the menu for tonight's dinner. Someone must plan for buying the ingredients and choosing the recipes. Finally, someone must prepare the ingredients, cook the food, and serve the meal. It may be that the same person performs all of these tasks, or they may be done by a team of people.

Get MAD!

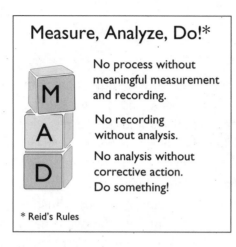

Measure, Analyze, Do!*

M

A

D

No process without meaningful measurement and recording.

No recording without analysis.

No analysis without corrective action.
Do something!

* Reid's Rules

Measurement plays a unique role for each of these three points of view—direction setting, planning, and doing. One of the authors, Robert Reid, encountered this uniqueness while working in a chemical plant. He developed three rules—measure, analyze, and do (MAD): There should be no process without meaningful measurement and recording, no recording without analysis, and no analysis without corrective action.

Measure

We worked with a group at an insurance company. The group consisted of customer service agents, claims adjusters, managers, and the vice-president of finance, who met to discuss how they could use measurement to help run their operation. Part of their job was recording the time it took to process an application or a claim. Stuart, the vice-president, asked how long it took to record the data. Carol, a claims adjustor, said "Five to ten minutes of every hour." Stuart responded, "How do you get all of your other work done if you have to spend so many minutes of every hour writing numbers on your log sheet?" Many in the room were shocked by Carol's response: "Sometimes I wait till the end of the day to fill out the log sheet, but quite often I log in all the data before I start the day's work." Stuart immediately asked, "How can you possibly do that?" Carol replied, "I have a magic pencil. It has all the numbers in it!"

From Carol's point of view, this answer made perfect sense because she believed she had two jobs. The first job was to evaluate and process claims; the second was to write little numbers on paper to make reports. She had no idea what one job had to do with the other, but she was paid equally for doing both. Being a good sport, she divided her time between processing claims and writing numbers on log sheets.

Analyze

Logging numbers doesn't really help anyone unless the data is meaningful and someone has time to analyze the data and look for patterns. Stuart asked Carol what she did with the log sheets and all the recorded data. She responded that she handed her log sheets to her supervisor, Anne. Stuart turned to Anne and asked what she did with the data, expecting that she would describe how she analyzed it and looked for patterns. Anne gave Stuart a strange look and responded, "All of my claims adjustors give me data sheets. I pile them on my desk and wait until the pile is nearly ready to tip over. Then I throw the bottom three-fourths away." Carol laughed: "I thought that was what happened, since it doesn't seem to matter what numbers I put on the log sheets as long as I turn them in every day."

Do

If you are going to study processes and activities, seeing patterns and gaining insights is of little value unless you use that information to improve your processes and activities. Measurement has a unique and special role in helping set direction, do planning, and achieve implementation.

The Measurement Chain

James Harrington has developed 11 questions (which we call the Eleven W's) that will help you think about the rules of measurement. The questions can be developed into a *measurement chain* that provides an easy way to make sure you are being efficient and effective. The questions are these:

1. Why should you measure?
2. Where should you measure?
3. What should you measure?

4. When should you measure?
5. Who should be measured?
6. Who should do the measuring?
7. Who should provide feedback?
8. Who should audit?
9. Who should set business targets and standards?
10. Who should set challenge targets or goals?
11. What should be done to solve problems?

Answer these 11 questions for your product or your process. A product may be a service that you provide, such as check cashing, or it may be a physical object, such as a computer.

Another way to develop a measurement chain is by making a list or chart using the following headings:

▶ Key success factors

Key success factors are things that are critical to your success. If you achieve your key success factors, you will be successful in what you are attempting. If you do not achieve them, you will not be successful.

▶ Definition of *excellence*

This sublist or column states what you mean by *excellence* for this product or service.

▶ How you know

The third sublist or column describes how you will know you have achieved excellence or how you will measure the result.

▶ Target

The fourth sublist or column specifies your goal or the target that you are aiming for.

▶ Current performance

The fifth sublist or column describes your current level of performance, measured by any or all of the following:

— *Timeliness*

The data should be up-to-date. Timely information enables you to meet present and anticipated needs.

— *Reliability*

Reliability enables you to factor the data into your decisions.

— *Efficiency and pertinence*

The information should meet but not exceed your needs. The cost to develop the information should not outweigh its value.

— *Responsibility*

The data must relate to the needs of those involved and be presented at an organizational level that is consistent with their responsibilities and span of control.

— *Exceptions*

The data generated may indicate situations that go beyond your expected norms. This type of information identifies exceptions or potential trouble spots.

—*Compliance*

The data meets predetermined reporting needs of the organization.

—*Comparison*

The data provides ratios and internal comparisons for evaluation.

► Gap

The sixth sublist or column identifies the gap between what you want to do and what you are doing.

The example shows the measurement chain used by a fast-food restaurant.

Measurement Chain

Key Success Factors	Definition of Excellence	How You Know	Target	Current Performance	Gap
• Hot	• Food is at appropriate temperature	• Measure	• Hamburger 125° Coffee 180°	• Hamburger 121° Coffee 182°	• Hamburger +4° Coffee −2°
• Tastes good	• Pleasing to palate	• Talk to customer	• 8 on survey	• 6.7 on survey	• −1.3 on survey

Different Types of Numbers

Using numbers to help you make better decisions involves a lot more than the arithmetic and calculations needed to manipulate them. Numbers occur in different contexts and mean different things to different people.

One reason that numbers have different meanings is that they come in two basic varieties. The first variety is called *attribute data*. For instance, "Did you enjoy the food at a fast-food restaurant?" The answer is yes or no. The food was either enjoyable or it was not enjoyable.

From now on, we will use this symbol to highlight a definition. All of the definitions so marked can be found in the glossary, along with some other terms that we think are important.

Attributes are things that are only counted, not measured.

In a manufacturing process, the number of rejected parts is an attribute. The number of defects in a part is an attribute. Attribute data does not tell you too much—it only counts, it does not measure. You know a certain number of parts failed, but you don't know how much they varied from specifications. Attribute numbers come from counting. For example, to determine how often you were satisfied with the service in a restaurant you count the number of times you liked your dinner or got what you wanted. How many times did your car not start last winter?

The second variety of numbers is called *variable data,* which results when variation is measured against a known standard. (How long was the bed? It was 6 feet, 4 inches long. How much did your steak weigh? It weighed 12 ounces.) Variable data is collected through measurement and requires a standard frame of reference such as units of length, weight, time, pressure, temperature, and the like.

Variable numbers come from either end results or the process that produces end results. You can measure the product, the goods, or the services you get when you are done, or you can look at the process that generated the end result. Variable data tells you considerably more about the product and is much more likely to lead you to the causes of variation. Variable data is usually more costly, time-consuming, and difficult to obtain. It doesn't help much to find out your product is bad if, by the time you get the numbers, the customer is already upset.

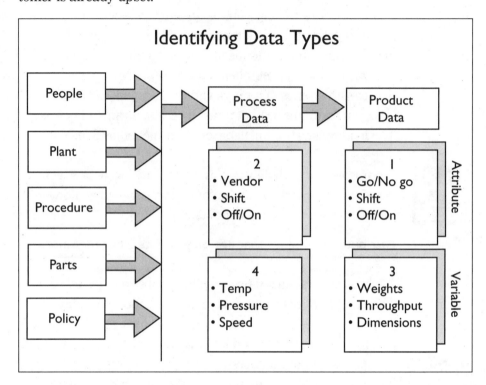

The illustration shows how to identify data types and clarifies the difference between attribute data and variable data. Let us use a fast-food restaurant as an example. The restaurant owner wants to know how often customers are satisfied with their meals. This is attribute data, as shown in box 1, because the number of times people liked their meals is counted.

The head chef manages the kitchen, plans the cooking, and also plans the serving process. The chef is concerned with both the product and the process. The chef's concerns, shown in boxes 2 and 3, include whether the right people are on duty, whether the right cooking methods are used, and whether the food is the right temperature when it is served. The chef is concerned about the attribute data concerning the back-office process and the variable data concerning the meal.

The French-fry cook is concerned with having the right amount of French fries and not burning them. That person's concerns are shown in box 4.

With this variety of concerns, it is no wonder that there is confusion in a restaurant or any other endeavor. The person who cooks the dinner has a different point of view than the person who plans the dinner, who has different point of view than the person who decides what to include on the menu. Different points of view result in different meaningful numbers and different insights into how well the enterprise is being run.

A simple set of drawings shows the relationship between product and process; attribute and variable data; and setting direction, planning, and doing. To make effective decisions, you need a way to do all three in concert.

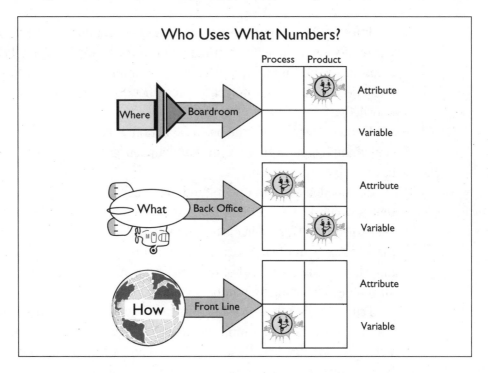

Why Use Numbers?

Numbers are the most common form of facts that we deal with on a regular basis; they are frequently called data. You are often asked to provide data to someone. Data is of little use alone, just as a single number or fact is meaningless. For instance, if we give you a variable number like 75, what does that mean? If we give you attribute data like "hot," what does that mean? It is mere data. It is a fact. It provides no information. For data to be useful, it must be made into information.

The most important figures are those that are unknown and unknowable. What about the multiplying effects of a happy customer, in either manufacturing or service? Is that in your figures? What about the multiplying effect of an unhappy customer? Is that in your figures?

W. Edwards Deming

Information provides answers to such questions as what, when, and where. If we say the temperature in your refrigerator is 75° or there is a full moon in the sky tonight, you have some information that you can use to make decisions. Using information together with your experience gives you knowledge.

Knowledge provides the basis for action. It answers the question of how something happens. If you find that your refrigerator is not plugged in, you have the basis for action.

Knowledge leads to understanding, which allows you to determine why things occur. Understanding leads to wisdom, which enables people to develop theories. Wisdom leads to comprehension, which provides the basis for the advancement of civilization. This hierarchy could be expanded to many more levels; however, most of the time, data, information, and knowledge are all you need when using numbers.

Data usually relates to short time periods such as hours or days. Information takes longer to compile and covers longer time spans, such as several weeks. Knowledge usually is only gained and relevant over a month or two. Because most of what you do focuses on how it is done, knowledge is usually sufficient to make most decisions.

Planning requires understanding, which usually takes one to five years to develop. Direction setting is best done with the aid of your wisdom and comprehension. Direction setting has long-term implications and should address a long time span. Unfortunately, there are no direct correlations among data, information, knowledge, understanding, wisdom, and comprehension. The broader your view of the issues, the better your decision-making process will be. Don't limit yourself to mere data and fact-based decisions. Remember, there is more than one way of looking at things. Let questions be your guide. Ask the right questions from the right points of view as you focus on data and information. The other points of view are harder, but they yield better and longer-lasting results.

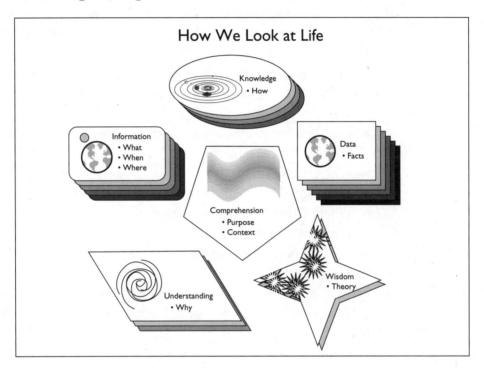

The Importance of Numbers

Using numbers to help make decisions is important for many reasons.

▶ Numbers focus your attention on whether or not you are attaining your goal. In other words, are you effective in doing what you set out to do?

▶ Numbers show how efficiently you are using your resources to get where you want to go.

▶ Numbers help you set goals and monitor your progress toward your goals.

▶ Numbers provide input and insights that help you analyze and understand why things are as they are.

▶ Numbers identify and point out opportunities for change and indicate situations where things should be left alone.

▶ Numbers can connect people, processes, and ideas and give everyone a sense of accomplishment. We all like to keep score. Imagine playing golf without keeping score—the game would be entirely different.

Before you collect any data, you should understand its purpose. Knowing the purpose leads to collection of the right data and to the best organization of the data. As you prepare to collect data, answer the following questions:

▶ What is the purpose of the data collection?
▶ Have the specific data parameters been identified?
▶ Is this effort an unnecessary duplication of something that has been done already?
▶ Has the effort been adequately coordinated with those of other organizations that are affected?
▶ Who is to collect the data?
▶ When should the data be collected?
▶ Where should the data originate?
▶ What forms will be used?
▶ Where will the data be retained?
▶ How long will the records be kept?
▶ How long does it take for the data to replace itself?
▶ Who is responsible for coordinating the effort?
▶ Is any training required?
▶ Is the purpose of the data collection clearly understood by everyone involved?
▶ To whom will the report be addressed?
▶ Who will prepare the final report?
▶ Has the budget authorization for the effort been coordinated?

Typically, variable data is richer and yields more insights than attribute data. Some simple questions can be used to clarify the differences between attribute and variable data.

Attribute Data	**Variable Data**
▶ Did the package arrive on time?	▶ How long did it take to deliver the package?
▶ Was the report turned in on schedule?	▶ How many hours early or late was the report?
▶ Is the car's engine efficient?	▶ How many miles per gallon does your car get?

How to Collect Data

One of the easiest and most effective ways to gather data is to use a check sheet. You can use this tool in a number of different situations—for instance, to gather data for later analysis, to find out how often something is happening, to find out what kinds of problems are arising, or to ascertain that something you believe is occurring is in fact taking place. The observations you take (your data samplings) should be as random as possible. The check sheet is a good starting point for solving most problems.

If you have answered the preceding questions about your data, you are ready to design your check sheet. We have included a check sheet that one of the authors used to improve his golf game. After deciding that he needed variable data, he designed the check sheet and used it to collect data about his game.

Check Sheet: Glen's Golf Game

	Slice	Hook	Wrong club	Looking up	Wiff	Bad grip	Other
Right distance		卌					|||
Too short	卌 ||	||	|||	卌	卌 ||	||	||||
Too long							||	
Off target	||||				||||		卌

With the proper preparation, data collection can provide the significant facts that you need to make decisions, solve problems, and develop objectives. Judgment, common sense, and consensus are still vital to the decision process, but these should be based on the collected data.

Being effective and getting the right results is far more important than being efficient and minimizing resources. It is much more important to do the right thing than to do the wrong thing efficiently.

Interpretation of data is more important than the data itself. How you use the data determines how useful it will be to you. Data can help you set direction. It can be used in planning or in doing.

Before collecting any data or numbers, you need to consider these basic ideas:

▶ Will the data collected help me see patterns?

▶ Can I arrange the data and find the patterns?

▶ Do not set out with a closed mind.

▶ Don't collect data unless you are willing to learn something from it.

▶ Don't assume you know what is happening in your process. Even the simplest of processes entails many subtle, variable interactions.

▶ Will you be present to observe the environment and the physical conditions when the data is collected?

▶ There is no good substitute for the adage that seeing is better than being told.

If you measure what you speak of and can express it by a number, you know something about your subject; but if you cannot measure it, your knowledge is meager and unsatisfactory.

Lord Kelvin

Just for Fun

Lora, the vice-president of procurement, just gave you a gallon jar. There are two bugs in the jar. Every minute, the number of bugs doubles. Assume the jug is filled in half an hour. Lora wants to know how long it will be before the jug is only half filled. She also needs to know how many bugs the full jug will contain.

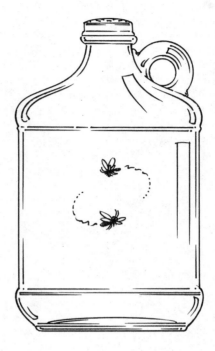

If you would like to check your answer, the solution is in Appendix B.

2

Patterns

Insights into the Way Things Are

Introduction

To learn from numbers, you must look for and recognize patterns. This is more important than collecting numbers. This chapter defines the patterns you will encounter when you use numbers to help you make better decisions. Large numbers of measurements tend to assume recurring, mountain-like shapes. The locations and spreads of these data mountains gives us clues about why things are as they are. These patterns also help us determine what we can do about the underlying causes of the patterns.

Spread or variation of results is of primary concern for many people and processes. Understanding variation is the first step toward controlling variation. We have studied thousands of processes and noticed several patterns appearing again and again. We have assigned a name to each of these patterns and present them here as examples to guide your decision making. We are sure the list is not complete; please add your own patterns from your world.

Recognizing Patterns

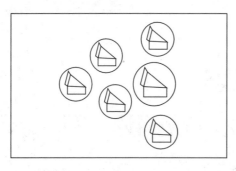

Throughout life, everyone makes decisions by recognizing and using patterns. Usually, however, you are not conscious of doing so. Let's start with a simple example: You're in front of the pie selection in the cafeteria. Aha! Just what we expected. You reach for the biggest piece. That's great—it shows that you understand the first principle of pattern recognition: Even a very good product or service will show an inherent variability if you have a measuring method sensitive enough to detect the variation. (There is a whole science of pattern recognition called statistics that we will get to later.)

But wait a minute! How do you know that you've chosen the biggest piece? Maybe by looking at the pieces you can classify them as big and little; however, we bet that you couldn't arrange a hundred pieces in order of size just by looking at them!

Let's go back into the kitchen, away from the eyes of curious customers, and weigh a hundred pieces of pie. We'll use a scale that will weigh each piece

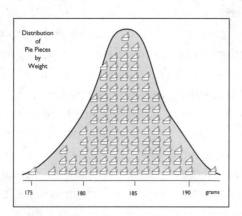

to the nearest gram (.035 ounces). You weigh the pieces, and we will plot them on a chart.

Now look at the chart. It shows the distribution of the weights of the pie pieces. Of course, you were right about there being big and little pieces. Observe that the number of pieces of pie varies from the smallest to the largest in a fairly smooth, regular, and symmetrical pattern. We have drawn a curve and shaded the area that very closely fits this particular distribution.

What do you think would happen if we measured a different group of a hundred pieces? In fact, we would get a very similar pattern in any group that we picked. This is a pattern that repeats itself endlessly, not only in pieces of pie but in most products and services. This pattern even repeats itself in nature.

We could show you hundreds of patterns like this. The measurements might be in inches, millimeters, hours, seconds, punctuation marks, or typing errors. They might include all sorts of items and all kinds of measurements. There is always an inherent variability, provided we have a measuring instrument sensitive enough to find the variations. These variations usually follow the same bell-shaped pattern, called the normal curve.

The greatest obstacle to the use of numbers is the mistaken idea that they are too difficult. In fact, they are most common. Everything varies. If you have enough data or numbers gathered through observation, you will find that eventually a pattern emerges. This pattern has a fancy name: It is called a histogram or frequency distribution.

A **histogram** or **frequency distribution** is a window that lets you envision or see what is happening.

You never have perfect data; all you ever have are some of the numbers. You never weigh every piece of pie. When you go to a doctor and have your blood tested, the technician takes a sample or some of your blood. That sample provides an indication of whether you are healthy or have a disorder.

The challenge in using numbers to make decisions is to recognize the patterns, understand them, and find out what is really going on. An interesting example from World War II helps makes this point. In 1943, Allied planes were bombing the Axis powers on a regular basis. When each bomber returned from its bombing run, a technical sergeant with a clipboard would walk around the aircraft and make a tick mark on a line drawing indicating where there was a bullet hole. The tool he used is called a measles chart.

A **measles chart** is a graphical representation of the object being studied with the data recorded on the image of the object.

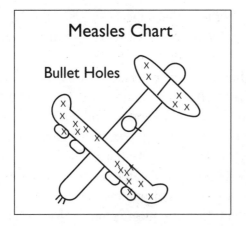

Measles Chart

Bullet Holes

This pictorial representation of data on the aircraft was then sent to the United States, where the planes were being produced. The engineers identified patterns in the hits and used this data to reinforce the aircraft and produce a better bomber. If you had been one of the designers and seen a pattern like this one, what would you have recommended? (Our recommendation is to join the Navy.) Where would you increase the armor plate on the aircraft? From which locations would you remove the strategic or vulnerable parts? Where would you put the strategic equipment?

Looking at patterns and coming to conclusions is not an automatic process. The designers did not put armor plate on the aircraft parts that showed many hits. Quite the opposite. The parts that showed no hits were the ones that received armor. The engineers reasoned that, as the aircraft flew over enemy territory, they probably received hits throughout the fuselage, the wings, and all other parts in equal proportions. The aircraft that returned came back to tell that they could withstand hits where they showed hits. The parts that showed no hits were vulnerable to attack; the planes that were hit in those places crashed in flames.

The interesting and important aspect of numbers is not the mechanics of doing the calculations or even plotting the graphics or making the charts. It is looking at the patterns, understanding the patterns, and taking action based on the patterns.

Shape

Distributions have shapes. Nature, left to its own devices, wants to produce a nice, smooth curve called the normal curve.

A **normal curve** is the bell shape that describes what happens when any system or process is left to operate by itself.

Line up a group of eighth-grade students by height or weight, and you will get a nice, smooth normal curve. Track your car's mileage per gallon, and you will get a normal curve. Measure the time it takes to get to work over 30 days, and most likely you will have another normal curve.

However, sometimes the top of the curve is not in the middle; the curve has a bubble on the left- or right-hand side. The fancy name for this pattern is *skewed.*

The normal law of error stands out in the experience of mankind as one of the broadest generalizations of natural philosophy. It serves as the guiding instrument in research in the physical and social sciences and in medicine, agriculture, and engineering. It is an indispensable tool for the analysis and the interpretation of the basic data obtained by observation and equipment.

W. J. YOUDEN

A **skewed distribution** occurs when the top of the normal curve is not in the middle. There is a bubble on either the left or the right side of the curve.

A curve can be skewed either to the left or to the right. When a curve is skewed, the data is trying to tell you something. The numbers indicate that something has occurred to cause this skewing of the pattern. If you think about it, you can probably puzzle out why the data is skewed to the left or the right. The curve does not tell you why this is so; it just gives you a signal to think about the reasons behind the pattern.

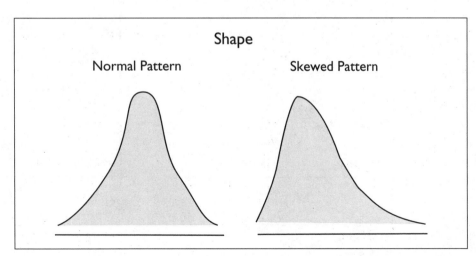

Accuracy

Sometimes a curve or pattern or histogram or distribution above or below the target. Here's a simple example. Suppose you are manufacturing M&M® candies, and your goal is to put 28 candies in each bag. When you count the number of candies in each bag, you find that the curve is shifted to the right. This means that you are putting too many candies in most bags.

A distribution not only has a shape, it has a location.

Location refers to how well the distribution is centered on a target.

When a distribution is centered on a target, it is considered accurate. For instance, the distribution for the M&Ms shows that you are giving most customers more candy than they are paying for. The distribution shows that you are not on target. A distribution can show that you are on target, below the target, or above the target.

The **target** is the exact quantity or quality that you are aiming for.

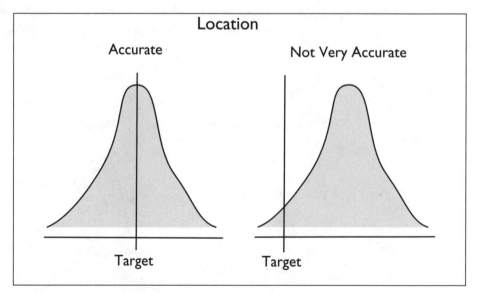

Spread

A distribution has another pattern that is important; it is called spread.

Spread is the difference between the high and low values in the group of data that you are measuring.

When you collect data and record observations, they can be very uniform or extremely varied. You can have numbers that are very close to each other (low of 160, high of 170) or a long way from each other (low of 63, high of 270).

When you have many numbers that are the same, your distribution is very precise. When you have many different numbers, the distribution is less precise.

Precision is the uniformity of the spread of the numbers in your data sample.

For instance, temperatures in Jacksonville, Florida, are very uniform when compared to temperatures in Bangor, Maine. Some distributions are very precise: They are very uniform and produce many numbers that are the same. Some distributions have greater spread or variety and produce many numbers that are different.

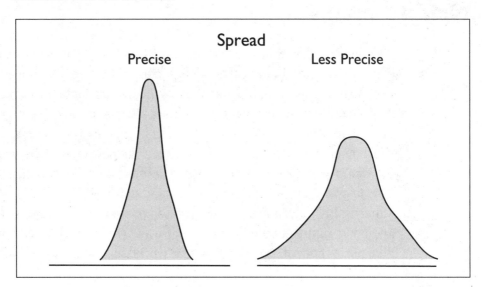

Variation

Distributions show variation. Variation is good or bad only in relation to some requirement.

Variation is the extent to which things differ, one to the next.

A requirement is what you want to have happen. In most life situations, there are desired outcomes or requirements. For instance, if you order a meal in a restaurant, you would like to have the food arrive within a certain time, within certain temperature limits, and with a certain portion size. Any requirement or specification has two limits. The lower limit is the least that you will accept; the upper limit is the most that you will pay for or accept. The target is your desired outcome. When results fall between the lower limit and the upper limit, the process is capable of meeting your requirements. If part of the curve or bubble falls outside the boundaries of your lower and upper limits, the process is not capable of satisfying you. Often, results are just not consistent with your requirements. There is too much variation to fit between the upper and lower specifications. This results in inefficiency.

Typical Patterns

As you collect data in your world and look at patterns, some patterns will occur more often than others. This section describes 14 common patterns that we have seen after looking at many, many distributions. We have also included some anecdotes that go with the patterns.

You may not find all of these patterns in your analyses, and you may identify different patterns. However, we are certain that you will observe some patterns, and we hope that the stories will be interesting. Your challenge is to look at your world to see what patterns occur and what you can do about those patterns. Before you read the description of a pattern, look at its illustration and try to figure out why it looks that way. After you have read the description, try to think of something in your world that has a similar pattern.

Our 14 patterns are all histograms. Histograms are used primarily to show patterns that result from processes, to help people make decisions about what is occurring in their processes, and to help them focus on what to improve for greater efficiency. In each histogram, you should look for the bar that is higher than the others. Also look for overall patterns that the bars form. The names of the patterns reflect their shapes.

Normal with Defects

The first pattern is a normal curve that occasionally produces some defects and thus is not capable of meeting the requirements. This is called a normal curve because the tallest bar is nearly in the center of the target, and the bars form a bell-shaped curve (just like the distribution of pie pieces on page 18).

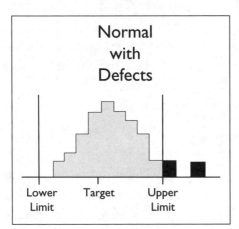

We first observed this distribution in a beer-bottling plant. While walking through the bottling plant, we noticed a gentleman sitting in a chair in a corner of a very large, three-story room. Bottles of beer were coming through the room on a production line. The bottles were filled with beer, a cap was applied to each bottle, and the bottles were labeled. The bottles were moving very rapidly. After watching the process for several minutes, we wondered why there was only one individual in the room. We patiently waited for the man in the corner to do something. About 35 minutes later, there was an enormous BOOM. One of the bottles had been overfilled; when pressure was applied to the cap, the bottle exploded, and pieces of glass came cascading down through the machine. The man stood up, got a broom, walked over, and swept up the broken glass. He put the broken pieces in the trash can and went over and sat down again. His job was to clean up the mess when overfilled bottles exploded.

Action called for: Reduce variation.

Absolute Limits

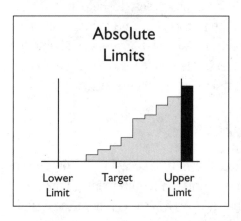

The second pattern is a distribution skewed with an absolute limit beyond which it will not go. Many kinds of processes produce absolute limits. For instance, it is physically impossible to buy a cup of coffee that is hotter than 212°F, the boiling point of water. At a higher temperature than that, the water boils away. Nature has provided all kinds of absolute limits beyond which we will not get numbers in normal circumstances. The temperatures in cups of coffee coming out of a restaurant should be close to the target value, not the upper absolute limit. Missing the target value can be very expensive. This pattern has cost some businesses millions of dollars in lawsuits because of coffee that was hotter than the customers wanted it.

Action called for: Know and understand the limit.

Bimodal with Defects

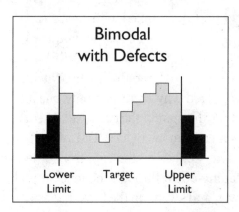

This pattern shows a bimodal distribution that produces defects. We call it a bimodal distribution because it includes two different bars that are very tall. Each of the two bars seems to have its own normal distribution. In this pattern, results are sometimes too small and sometimes too large. We saw this pattern when we observed the merging of two banks. The time it took to get a loan was different at the two banks because they used different processes. Both banks had to agree to use the same loan process so that they could provide loans within the same time frame.

Action called for: Create a single distribution.

Cut Off at Limit

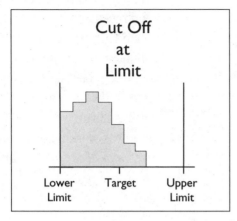

This pattern is another example of a skewed distribution. It arouses suspicion because the numbers end at the lower requirement level. Because the numbers end abruptly, we say this pattern is cut off at the limit. This pattern occurs when someone is working very hard to meet requirements and stopping results from falling below the lower limit. We saw this pattern in an insurance company concerning the length of time it took to issue a policy. The cutoff at the lower limit was due to a mandatory waiting period.

Action called for: Understand the cut-off limit.

Centered within Limits

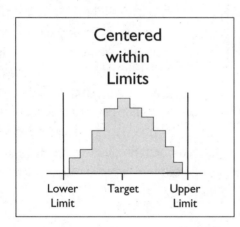

This is an almost perfect pattern. It is what you like to see—a process that is centered and gives the expected results time after time. This pattern is normally distributed, with the tallest bar in the center of the target and the rest of the bars between the lower and the upper requirements.

Action called for: Have standard operating procedures to ensure these results consistently.

Gaptoothed

This pattern shows a process that is gaptoothed. At many points, the bars or data are not touching each other. Whoever or whatever is producing this result

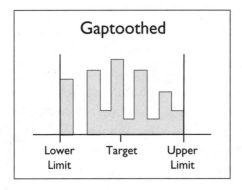

has a favorite spot where it likes to run. We observed this pattern in a piece of equipment with gauges labeled in 5-pound increments (i.e., 5, 10, 15, and 20 pounds). It was almost impossible to get any other settings. Each operator had his or her favorite settings, and the results clearly showed which operator was working on the machine.

Action called for: Improve control over processes.

Centered with Defects

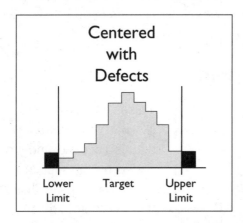

This pattern shows a process that is centered on the desired result but with too much variation. It is very similar to the Centered within Limits pattern. The difference is that the pattern goes beyond the upper and lower limits. Using a process depicted by this pattern, you cannot help but sometimes make things that are not right. The variations in the process need to be reduced so that the output is more uniform. We see this pattern often. Frequently, the items that fall outside the specifications are separated out and either scrapped or reworked.

Action called for: Reduce variation.

Bimodal within Limits

This pattern is similar to the Bimodal Distribution. The difference is that the process meets the requirements of the upper and lower limits. The customer's measurement system may not see unsatisfactory results, but the customer may experience problems within his or her own processes. The difficulty with processes that produce this pattern is that they typically yield satisfac-

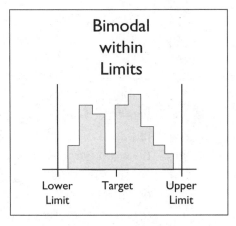

tory results. It is easy to ignore the fact that two different things are occurring, but it is important to identify what is causing the problem. You need to determine whether the pattern is due to two operators, two different strategies, two pieces of equipment, or some other discrepancy. We observed this pattern in a pharmacy, where we were measuring the time it took to fill a prescription. Our findings showed the difference between times it took for the two pharmacists to fill prescriptions.

Action called for: Create a single distribution.

Off Center out of Limits

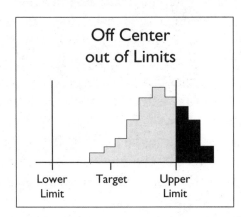

This pattern shows a process that is off center and is producing defective results. Even though the pattern is off center, it has a normal distribution. Typically, a single adjustment can center the process and move it back between the upper and lower limits. This action reduces the number of defects being produced. If you see this pattern, be certain to find the real reason why the process is off the target. Don't just change the process without knowing why you must change it.

Action called for: Adjust the process.

Dual Distribution

In this pattern, a dual distribution, there are obviously two of something. An example of a dual distribution occurred in a plant manufacturing plastic

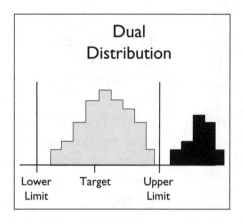

Dual Distribution

Lower Limit   Target   Upper Limit

packaging trays for chicken. The customer, a chicken packer, was very concerned that the trays be of uniform thickness. The packer had automated his process. The chicken was placed on the tray and wrapped in plastic wrap. Sometimes the plastic wrap would break the tray and cause the production line to go down. The packer complained to the tray manufacturer of breakage.

An empowered team of operators on B shift heard of the complaint. They took it upon themselves to recalibrate the machines on their shift to a thicker setting: They would make extra-thick trays that would never break. They did not inform the other shifts of their reason for the change, so the A and C shifts recalibrated the machines to the old specification each day. The black pattern in the histogram represents the thick trays that B shift was making; the gray pattern is the regular trays that A and C shifts were making. While this was going on, there were actually two factories in one. One factory (B shift) was making the super-thick trays, and the other factory (A and C shifts) was making the regular trays. The result was disastrous. The chicken packer received some of the extra-thick trays and recalibrated all his equipment to handle them. When the regular trays from the other two shifts came in, instead of one or two trays jamming up the packing process, most of the trays jammed the process. The whole chicken processing plant went down. Generally, dual distributions indicate that things must be improved.

Action called for: Understand and remove the distributions that are out of the specification limit.

Result by Sorting

We call this pattern result by sorting because the bars stop abruptly at the upper and lower limits. Remembering that every process will seek a normal curve if left to itself, you should be very suspicious about what happens to

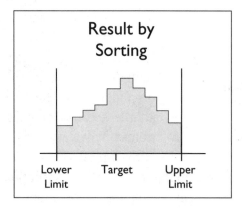

the missing numbers of the normal curve. Here, for some reason, the too-large and too-small results are not getting out of the facility. This is a very common but very expensive pattern. Sorting can prevent most defects from reaching the customer, but it costs a lot of money and time. *Action called for: Reduce variation.*

Flinching

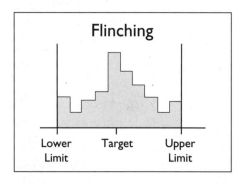

We call this pattern flinching because it almost looks like someone raising his or her shoulders. Some people think it looks a little like Batman's hat because the edges stick up very high. That Batman's cowl, or what we call flinching, indicates a pattern that is the opposite of Result by Sorting. Flinching is usually a result of mismeasuring or mislabeling to improve production. For example, when the lower limit is 19 and the result is 18, you let it go because it is close enough. You might label all of the 38s as 37, which is the upper limit. This simple change will allow you to increase production; it may also cost you your customer. This is the same as result by sorting, except that defective items are going to the customer as if they were good.
Action called for: Reduce variation.

Heart Cut

This pattern appears to be missing a whole chunk of data. The numbers in the center probably existed at one time and went somewhere else. Someone has cut the heart out of this distribution. This pattern is interesting because

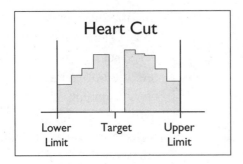

it shows that sorting is also occurring. Some preferred customer may be getting all the prime meats or the center part of our distribution. Some discounted operator may be getting all the seconds or culls at the extremes. We experienced this pattern with an electronics manufacturer, who was shipping all the parts from the center of the distribution to a maker of medical equipment. These parts commanded a premium price because they were in a critical environment. The parts still visible in the pattern were shipped to an automotive manufacturer, and those that fell outside of the lower and upper limits were sold to an offshore manufacturer.

Action called for: Reduce variation. Charge more for the heart cut.

Off Center within Limits

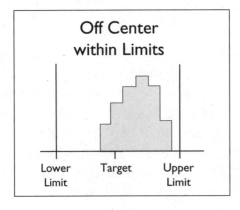

By no means is this meant to be the last pattern; there are probably thousands and thousands of patterns that you can find in your world. This process is capable of doing what you want, but it is not centered. It is shifted a bit to the right. You could adjust the process and bring it back so that it is centered right on the desired results; you may or may not choose to do so at this time.

Action called for: Adjust the process.

No matter how many or what kind of numbers you collect, they will form some sort of pattern. We have shown you two pictorial or graphical ways to look at data—curves and histograms. When you look at data graphically, you can identify the patterns that are significant.

The best way to see patterns is to look at the distributions of data. We have shown how these distributions form curves or bar charts that display different patterns. The bar charts are called histograms and should be easy to interpret. Each bar should be the same width, and there should be no space between bars. Histograms are helpful because they

 ▶ Visually show the spread and distribution of the data,
 ▶ Provide an easy way to communicate what is happening with your process,
 ▶ Indicate that there is a problem with your process, and
 ▶ Help you to focus on what to improve.

Patterns provide clues for you to use. What you do about the patterns is up to you.

Just for Fun

Lori, the lead programmer, walked away from her work station and left her computer running. Ed the Wizard sneaked in and installed his new graphical security program on it. When Lori returned to work, she faced a predicament. She had to place the symbols into the proper portions of the hexagon, or her computer would not let her work. Where did she place the symbols in the blank hexagon? Why?

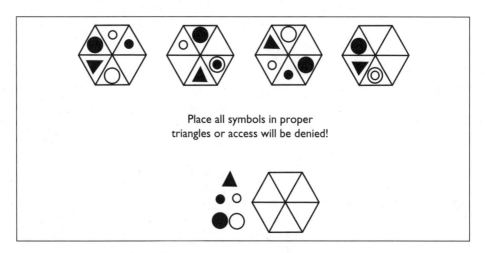

Place all symbols in proper
triangles or access will be denied!

If you would like to check your answer, our solution is in Appendix B.

3

Characterization

Using One Number to Represent a Group of Numbers

Introduction

Numbers are a universal language. To communicate effectively in this language, we must have a way to express a large quantity of numbers as one single number. This chapter will introduce you to descriptive statistics. Don't let the name scare you. You have used descriptive statistics all your life. Descriptive statistics uses a number of terms that you have already heard. The first one is *average*. Averaging is finding one number that represents or describes a group of numbers—average grades in a history class, average temperature in December in New England, and so forth. The list is endless. All of us use averages every day.

Other descriptive statistics terms include *mean, median,* and *mode.* These are all examples of measures of a central tendency or average. Measuring how things differ is the key to better decision making. Practical measures of variation are the range and the standard deviation. The importance of descriptive measures lies not in the calculations that you perform but in the information and insight you gain for use in decision making.

This chapter will end with a great story about shooting arrows to hit a target. The results of any process can be on or off target. Results also have a degree of precision; that is, they may be uniform or spread out. Understanding accuracy and precision takes a little practice, but it is worth the effort. We will make you comfortable with all of the pertinent terms in this chapter.

Math Terms and Names

Using numbers to make better decisions reduces the variability of your actions and processes. As you begin to recognize some of the patterns we described in the last chapter, you will become more comfortable using numbers on a daily basis. When you start talking with others who use numbers every day, you will hear some pretty mysterious-sounding terms. These terms are used in a lot of different ways. In fact, the variety of ways numbers can be used often leads to the feeling that you can prove anything you want with statistics. If you understand math terms, you will be able to avoid the traps that are easy to fall into.

We don't want to overload you with terminology, but there are some terms you should get familiar with. Following are the essential terms:

The **median** is the value of the middle item (or the average of the middle two items) when the data is arranged from the lowest to the highest number.

For example, if the ages of the last seven people hired are 21, 25, 26, 19, 21, 27, and 22, then the median (or middle) age is 22 years.

$$
\begin{array}{r}
19 \\
21 \\
21 \\
\text{Median} = 22 \\
25 \\
26 \\
27
\end{array}
$$

The **mode** is the single number that occurs most frequently in the data you have collected.

There are more 21-year-olds than any other age.

Mode = 21

The **mean** is the average of the numbers (data) you have collected. You find the mean by dividing the sum of all the numbers by the number of numbers you have collected. The mean (or average) is represented by the symbol $\bar{x}$; it is pronounced "X bar."

The sum of 161 divided by 7 equals the mean age of 23.

Age	Numbers Collected
21	Mary
25	Alick
26	Bob
19	Betty
21	Fred
27	Liz
22	Frank
161	

Mean = $161 \div 7 = 23$

The **range** is a measurement of the spread of the numbers or data you have collected. You find it by subtracting the lowest number from the highest number in your data.

27 years is the oldest; 19 years is the youngest. The difference is 8 years.

$$
\begin{array}{r}
27 \\
-19 \\
\hline
\text{Range} = \quad 8
\end{array}
$$

The **standard deviation** is a measurement of the total variability of the data. It is an average of deviations from the mean. Standard deviation also shows up very frequently as a symbol that looks like this: σ. This is a Greek letter used by mathematicians. It is pronounced "sigma."

The standard deviation of the ages of the new hires is 3 years. That is to say, on the average, a new hire's age will vary from the mean (23 years of age) by plus or minus 3 years.

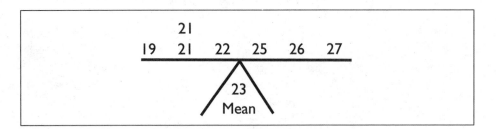

By now, either you are ready to shut this book and say that you will never be successful in using numbers, or you are curious enough to read another paragraph or two about how you can begin to use these terms and numbers in your daily life.

In the last chapter, we talked about patterns represented in bar charts or histograms that showed curves (normal, we hope). The following example is based on the pattern of a normal curve or histogram.

We looked at the height of soldiers in the United States Army. The average height of men in the army was 67.7 inches, but heights of individuals varied all the way from 60 to 76 inches. Sixty-eight percent were between 65.1 and 70.3 inches tall; 95 percent measured between 62.5 and 72.9 inches. You would seldom see a soldier over 75.5 inches tall. The army did not want men under 60 inches in height.

Do you suppose we got all those figures from a list of data? Well, not exactly. Here is the reference table we used. It tells us only two things about each height measurement. Using $\bar{x}$, we are able to ascertain that the average height is 67.7 inches. That is the mean or middle of the curve. It is the height of the largest percentage of men.

Human Proportions

Measurement	Men $\bar{x}$	Men σ	Women $\bar{x}$	Women σ
Height (standing)	67.7	2.6	62.5	2.4
Height (sitting)	36.0	1.3	33.9	1.2
Length of foot	10.1	1.0	8.2	.8
Arm span	69.9	3.1	62.4	2.7

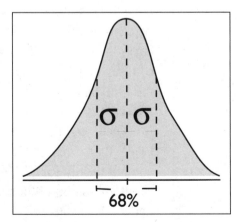

68%

The second thing the table tells us is variation in human proportions. The symbol σ is actually the Greek letter *sigma*. Remember, it is also called the standard deviation. If you want to get technical, it is the distance from the center to the place where the curve begins spreading out more than dropping down. If you knew enough about mathematics, you could use σ and $\bar{x}$ in the formula for the normal curve and compute the number of men between any two heights you might specify.

For most purposes, however, we are interested only in the points at one, two, and three standard deviations, measured from the center or target. If we measure a standard deviation on each side of the center of this curve, we have $\bar{x} \pm 1\sigma$, or 68 percent of the area between the lines drawn through these points. In other words, 68 percent of all of the data falls within the mean plus or minus one standard deviation. We will teach you how to use σ by simply adding, subtracting, multiplying, and dividing. It is not hard, and once you understand the operation, you can use a calculator or a computer to do the arithmetic for you.

Men's Heights

$$\pm \ 1\sigma = 2.6"$$

$$67.7 - 2.6 = 65.1"$$
$$67.7 + 2.6 = 70.3"$$

$$\pm \ 2\sigma = 2.6" \times 2 = 5.2"$$

$$67.7 - 5.2 = 62.5"$$
$$67.7 + 5.2 = 72.9"$$

$$\pm \ 3\sigma = 2.6" \times 3 = 7.8"$$

$$67.7 - 7.8 = 59.9"$$
$$67.7 + 7.8 = 75.5"$$

The table of human proportions tells us that the standard deviation for men's height is 2.6 inches. By using simple subtraction and addition, we determine that 68 percent of the men are between 65.1 and 70.3 inches tall.

Two standard deviations is 5.2 inches. Once again, using simple subtraction and addition, we know that 95 percent of the men are between 62.5 and 72.9 inches tall.

Three standard deviations is 7.8 inches. This table shows that 99.73 percent of the area of the normal curve is between -3σ and $+3\sigma$. We can say that practically all of the men will be between 59.9 inches and 75.5 inches.

There certainly are some men taller than 75.5 inches, but they amount to only 15 in 10,000. There is about the same proportion of men under 59.9 inches.

What have all these calculations to do with providing good service or making nuts and bolts or Jeeps or aspirin tablets (except, you say, that we are giving you a headache)? Now, be patient. Pretend that you are still in the army and are staying there until you learn something about probability. Suppose we could go down the street and measure the height of the next soldier who passes the door of this building. What odds would you give that he would be exactly 67.7 inches tall? That is the average, you know.

Of course you would have to give pretty big odds. Obviously, the soldier could be anywhere between 59.9 and 75.5 inches in height. You would certainly try to collect if he varied from the average by even one thousandth of an inch!

Instead, suppose we bet that the next soldier would be between 65.1 and 70.3 inches tall. How would you figure the odds? We have already given you the answer. Sixty-eight percent of all the soldiers are between 65.1 and 70.3 inches tall. There are 68 chances in 100 that the next soldier would be within those limits. I would have to give you odds of 68 to 32, or 2 to 1.

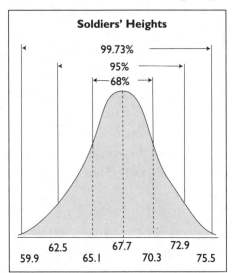

Ninety-five percent of all soldiers are between 62.5 and 72.9 inches, so the odds are 95 to 5, or 19 to 1, that the next man will be neither shorter than 62.5 inches nor taller than 72.9 inches. There are only 2.5 chances in 100 that he will be taller than 72.9 inches and 13.5 chances in 10,000, or 1 in 740, that he will be taller than 75.5 inches.

Let's go back to the world of business for another example. We want to cut a lot of Widgets exactly 2 inches long using our special Widget maker. (In case you do not know what a Widget is, refer to the illustration on the next page.) Yesterday we cut 500 Widgets. We measured them all very carefully and made a histogram of what we found. As you see, the Widget lengths vary in the bell-shaped pattern or normal curve. The mean is 2.00 inches, but individually the Widgets vary from 1.91 inches to 2.09 inches.

That is okay with our customers. Their specifications require an average of 2.00 inches, with a tolerance of plus and minus 0.15 inches. That means they will accept anything between 1.85 inches and 2.15 inches.

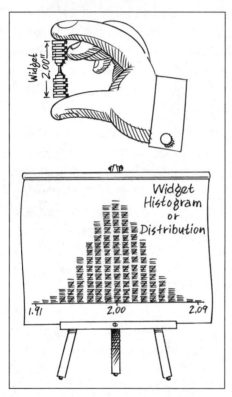

Our problem is to keep the cutting machine at the center of 2 inches and not let the individual pieces vary much more than they did in yesterday's lot. Please note that the same logic applies to non-Widget numbers such as the number of minutes required to process an invoice or the number of customers checked into a hotel during the day shift. We need to be accurate and precise to keep our customers happy. (We will discuss accuracy and precision in more detail later in the chapter.)

All of our Widgets were made at one time, on the same machines, by the same operator, and from the same lot of material, so we are quite sure that the pattern of their variation will almost exactly fit the normal curve. We also know that 99.7% of the widget variations will be within −3 and +3 standard deviations of the mean. That is a spread of 3 standard deviations—±3σ or 6σ in total.

As we teach you the arithmetic used in the book we will use Glen's daily commuting time. It would be a good thing for you to record your own travel time for 30 days and work through the arithmetic yourself.

Glen's times for the first 10 days are represented in the first row, days 11 through 20 in the second row, and days 21 through 30 in the third row.

```
58  57  60  55  57  55  55  64  56  71
61  57  62  58  77  59  58  52  54  48
72  63  60  57  55  57  45  59  57  58  min.
```

Record your travel times on a sheet of paper. You might want to number the days or use rows as we did to ensure that you know which times are associated with which days. To understand more fully how you can use numbers to make better decisions, practice the methods in each chapter using your travel times. What is the median of your travel times? What is the mode of your travel times? What is the range of your travel times? What is the standard deviation of your travel times?

Variation, Accuracy, and Precision

The way numbers differ is called variation. One goal in using numbers for making decisions is to hold the variation in your process to a minimum. Ideally, the mean of your process would be equal to your target.

Accuracy is how well numbers center on your target. Precision is how alike the numbers are. Precision and accuracy are two different ways of looking at numbers. A simple story of four friends shooting arrows at a bull's-eye illustrates the difference between accuracy and precision.

The first archer is Mary. She takes careful aim and shoots her 10 arrows at the center of the target. Mary's arrows all hit near the center of the target, so she is accurate; her arrows are all close to one another, so she is precise. She is a good shot.

Tom draws his bow and scatters his shots all about the target. Tom is not very precise; his shots are not very repeatable. What he does differs from shot to shot. However, on the average, he covers the target, so we can say he is accurate. This notion is hard for a lot of people to understand. Accuracy merely means centered on the target. You recall that we defined accuracy as attaining the center of the target.

Bill shoots his arrows, clustering his hits slightly above the target. Bill is precise; his shots are very repeatable. He is consistent. However, he is not on target, so he is not accurate.

Nina is just learning to use a bow and arrow. Nina's shots are erratic and far from the target. She is neither precise nor accurate.

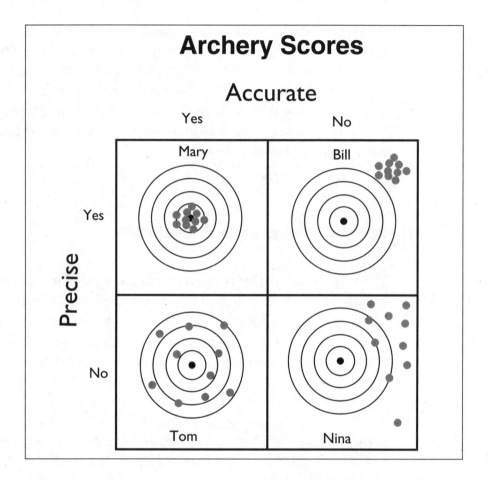

If the four friends are filling gallon cans of paint instead of shooting arrows, whose paint would you like to buy if your objective were to receive the quantity of paint that you ordered?

Mary would be the best selection because every can she filled would contain close to a gallon of paint—just what you asked for. You would not like to buy from Nina: You would never know what you were going to get, but you could be sure it would be wrong.

Suppose, now, that you cannot find Mary to buy from and you can avoid Nina. Would you rather buy from Bill or Tom?

Well, each has his advantages and disadvantages. Tom, at least on the average, would give you as much paint as you had paid for. Therefore, if you bought 100 gallons of paint from Tom, you would get a total of 100 gallons.

Some cans would have a bit too much and some too little, but the total would be correct. If you bought 100 gallons from Bill and all 100 were identical but each gallon were an ounce short, you would be short 100 ounces of paint. On the other hand, if each gallon were the same but each gallon had an ounce too much, you would have an extra 100 ounces. Many manufacturers say they would rather have a vendor like Bill even though he does not do exactly what they want. They always know what he does and can compensate by buying an extra gallon of paint.

The exciting thing about using numbers is that the answer is not in the numbers—it is in your use of the numbers. The answer is in recognizing the patterns, averages, and deviations and using them to your advantage. You must use the data to determine the appropriate decision for you.

Another way to view our archery scores would be to construct curves of the data.

Mary is accurate and precise. Her average and her mean are equal to the target. Her standard deviation is relatively small.

Bill is precise but not accurate. His average equals something other than the target, but his standard deviation is relatively small.

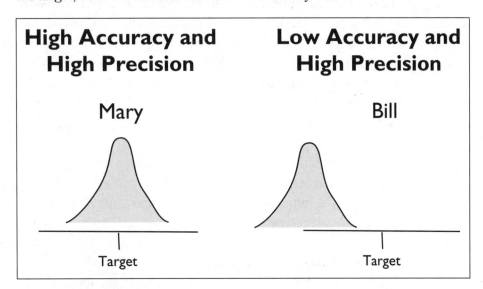

Tom is accurate. His average equals the target, and his standard deviation is greater than zero. He has variation. He lacks precision.

Nina is neither precise nor accurate. Her average is not equal to the target, and her standard deviation is greater than zero.

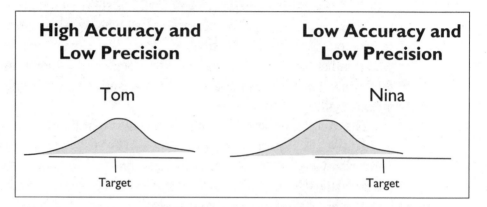

The best processes are on target and repeatable like Mary's. A highly accurate and precise process develops a nice single mountain of product.

Processes that vary a lot are like Tom's. Such a process yields a flat mountain of product that lacks precision though it is accurate. A lack of precision due to too much variation may be difficult to correct. Typically, an excess of variation must be improved with the help of management.

A process like Bill's is highly accurate and precise. It develops a nice single mountain of product; however, it is not centered on the target. It may in fact produce a lot of waste. It results in a service or product that your customer is not happy with. Such processes are not on target, though they are very consistent. If you lack accuracy, most likely there is a single special, assignable cause for that result. You need to adjust your process and bring it back to the target.

Processes like Nina's have neither accuracy nor precision. Such a process yields a flat mountain of product that is not centered on the target. This pattern requires immediate action by you and your management working together. Your customers will be very unhappy. They may turn to another vendor and never return if you do not make dramatic and significant changes.

Data should be used to find problems with processes, not with people. We have found that, when you look at what is causing an unacceptable data pattern, over 90 percent of the time the problem is a process problem, not a people problem.

It is helpful to think of your process as producing a large quantity of result. Your dilemma is that most customers do not see all of your products. They just see one product, and that one product is either good or bad as far as they are concerned.

For this reason, you must be very careful when you use averages. You must know what information you need so you can use your wisdom to improve your processes. Do not start by simply collecting all the data you can. When you understand your information requirements, you are ready to begin to collect data.

The key to using your data is to identify the pattern and decide what to do about it. You must

▶ Use the numbers to manage the accuracy and precision of your process.

▶ Remember that normal distributions are the result of random variability.

▶ Understand that lack of accuracy is easier to correct than lack of precision.

▶ Keep your process as simple as possible. Doing so will make the process easier to improve.

Just for Fun

Ed the Wizard has granted you the opportunity of a lifetime because you were able to help him fix his computer. The wizard has three identical treasure chests, each with two lids. He grants you one chance to open one lid to find immense wealth. He tells you that one treasure chest has immense wealth beneath both lids. One has immense wealth behind one lid and a lump of coal beneath the other. The last treasure chest has a lump of coal beneath each lid. You choose one lid and throw it open, only to find a lump of coal. What were your odds of finding the lump of coal?

Ed turns out to be a very nice wizard. He grants you a second chance. What are your odds of finding great wealth when you open the next lid?

The solution is in Appendix B.

4

Movement

Looking at Trends Over Time

Introduction

We are all moving in the same direction in our lives. That is, we are moving forward in time. Seeing and understanding change over time helps you control the future results of what you do. Historical data consists of measurements showing past performance. Past performance provides a window into the future. To take advantage of that window, you must be able to recognize recurring patterns. There are many tools to help you recognize them.

One tool that plots measurement data over time is called a run chart. A run chart helps you identify when intervention in a process is called for by revealing unusual patterns. The three most common patterns that require investigation are seven values going up or down in succession, seven values in succession falling on one side or the other of the average, and one extreme high or low spike occurring. This chapter takes a detailed look at each of these patterns, the reasons they might appear, and steps you can take to change them. Plotting data over time is an excellent first step in understanding a process. It is easy, simple, and quick.

Movement over Time

One number by itself is meaningless. Is 72°F good or bad? It depends. What do you want? What was the temperature an hour ago? Yesterday? Last week? In this chapter, we look at numbers over time. When you make data into a graphical display, distinct straight lines are easier for the eye to read than areas. Even though we have devoted a great deal of attention to bar charts or histograms, linear displays are better than divided bar charts for presenting data clearly. Bar charts are better than pie charts, and pie charts are better than written volumes.

Whatever type of display you use, when you are looking at movement over time, it is critical to remember that you are looking for long-term trends and patterns. If you focus only on short-term fluctuations, you will waste a great deal of time and energy overcontrolling and overcorrecting. We experienced this type of short-term focus at a paper mill where the plant manager focused on daily output.

The plant was supposed to produce 170 tons of paper every day. When the plant manager first arrived each day, he asked the production manager what the previous day's production had been. If the production had exceeded 170 tons, the plant manager was in a very good mood. If it stayed above 170 tons for two days in a row, he bought everyone sandwiches for lunch. However, if production was below 170 tons, he summoned all the mangers for an immediate meeting to find out what had gone wrong. The workers were always very tense, and production was constantly erratic.

After we convinced the plant manager to take a longer look at the output, production problems became less prevalent, and the workers' confidence increased. The tool that we used to help the plant manager was a run chart, a simple but helpful way to display data to make it easily understood.

Dd

This is a sample of the text for the definition, or these are more synonyms and usages that are commonly found in the English language.

A **run chart** merely plots the movement of something over a given period of time.

Run charts are the simplest of the numerical problem-solving tools to use and master. To make a run chart, you plot data points on a graph in the order in which the data becomes available over time. It is quite common to graph results of a process such as waste, errors, or efficiency as they vary over time. What you plot must be meaningful in terms of what your customer wants you to deliver. The time increment that you use to plot the data must be meaningful to the process. You can plot run charts in seconds, minutes, hours, days, or some longer or shorter increments. For instance, if you are plotting average rainfall per month in a given area, you will get only 12 data points in a year.

A run chart identifies trends or shifts in the output of a process. For example, when monitoring a process, you normally find equal numbers of points falling above and below the average. When seven data points fall on one side of the average, it indicates that a statistically unusual event has occurred. The average has changed for some reason, and you should investigate to find out why. Make any favorable shift a permanent part of the system or process; eliminate any unfavorable shift.

A second type of possible pattern is a trend of seven or more data points that steadily go up or down with no change in direction. You should expect neither the rising nor the falling pattern to happen randomly. You should investigate your process to discover what has caused these significant changes.

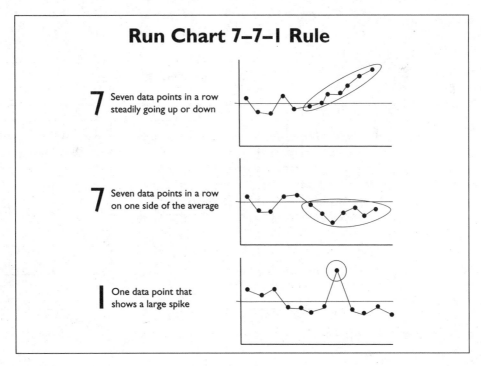

Run Chart 7–7–1 Rule

7 Seven data points in a row steadily going up or down

7 Seven data points in a row on one side of the average

| One data point that shows a large spike

In a third type of pattern, one data point falls significantly outside of the pattern. When the points are plotted, there appears to be a spike in the line. The spike can be either up or down. You should investigate the process to discover what had caused the spike.

Resist the temptation to tamper or overadjust your process every time you see a variation in data. Only significant changes like the three just described should cause you to implement a change.

When you prepare any type of chart, including run charts, don't be afraid to add comments. They usually provide the basis for analysis of patterns that you find in the data. The comments should include any unusual or significant events in the period being examined, such as a new operator working on a machine or a power outage affecting your computer.

The example is a run chart of Glen's commute time from page 42 for 30 days. Following are the times on which the chart is based.

Commute Times

58	57	60	55	57	54	55	64	56	71
61	57	62	58	77	59	58	52	54	48
72	63	60	57	55	57	45	59	57	58

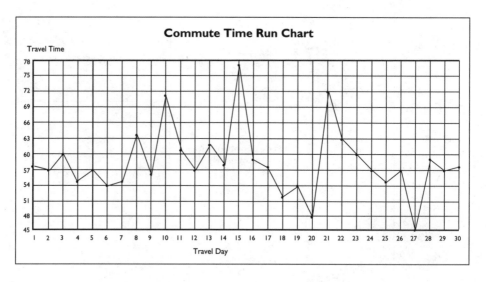

You may want to plot your commute times and look for patterns in your run chart.

Typical Run Chart Patterns

Plotting numbers over time reveals quite a few different patterns, and patterns provide information. Once you have information, you can use your wisdom to define the problem. After you have defined it, you will be able to develop many potential solutions. If you only see or generate one solution to a problem, you do not understand the problem. The following are patterns we have typically seen in run charts.

Trend

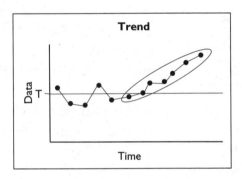

A trend is the pattern that emerges when seven or more values in a row go up or down. When this many data points go in the same direction, the change is probably not due to chance. The data is telling us that the process we are observing has shifted in some way. The shift can have any number of explanations. It may have happened because a part has worn out, summer has arrived and the outside temperatures are hotter, or some other reason. Unless you take action the trend will continue. If you do not act, your equipment may fail or your customers may become dissatisfied with your service or product. Your job when monitoring a process is to respond before the process totally breaks down.

Run

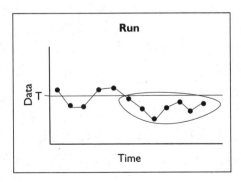

A run is a series of seven readings that fall either above or below the mean (average). A run typically occurs when a process is stuck at a new level. Let's look at making pies. If you weigh every pie and each pie is heavier than the average, you know something has changed. Perhaps you are using a different type of apple that has higher or lower water content. Perhaps a valve is opening wider and putting more filling in each pie. If a run occurs, you need to use your knowledge to detect what is causing the change.

Irregular Shifts

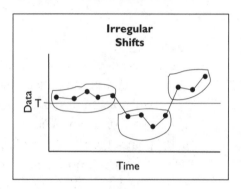

This pattern shows irregular shifts—times when the process runs above the average for a while, then shifts to another level and remains there for a while. The data then jumps to another level, or back to the original level. Quite often, shifts occur when different operators or different individuals run the process using different preferred settings.

Cycle

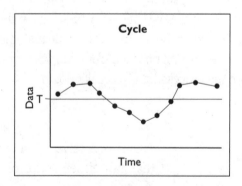

This pattern is the cycle. Life is full of ongoing cycles. For instance, a thermometer showing the ambient temperature outside a window would reflect the night-day temperature cycle. Most processes have natural cycles. The closer the cycle is to the target, the better your customer will like what you provide.

Sawtooth

The sawtooth pattern emerges when values jump back and forth from high to low on a regular basis. Typically, this pattern results from someone's tam-

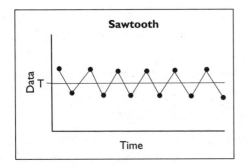

pering with or overcontrolling the process. A simple example is an inexperienced canoeist trying to navigate a stream and oversteering. The front of the canoe wobbles back and forth, pointing first toward the left bank, then toward the right bank.

Spike

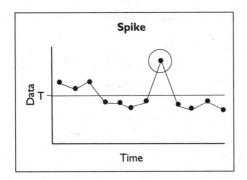

A spike is a single value that is extremely high or extremely low. Quite often, spikes are one-time occurrences. A spike is usually due to a transient event that does not repeat itself. Examine a spike carefully because it could indicate a potential major problem.

Even though the spike may not reappear, you need to understand why it occurred to prevent potential trouble. Spikes are often identified through comments written on run charts. Because the person who analyzes the pattern of the run chart may not be the one who recorded the data, these comments can be invaluable. (Recall MAD: measure, analyze, and do. The same person does not necessarily fulfill all three functions.)

Reasons to Use Data

There are three very important reasons for using data. The first is to find and correct problems with your processes. The second is to find opportunities for improvement. The third is to help you understand how well things are progressing. Charts are a simple, yet powerful tool that can help you make the best use of data. A chart requires no computer nor even a pocket calculator. All you need is a piece of paper and a pencil.

Most people think of what they do from at least two perspectives. The first perspective is movement over time. The second is the sum total of the results produced during a given period.

It may be difficult to visualize the histogram that would go with the corresponding run chart. To make it easier, imagine that each point on the run chart is a bead that can slide along a horizontal wire. As you rotate the run chart 90° degrees, the beads slide toward the lower end. In other words, the bottom of the run chart is turned and becomes the right side of the histogram. All the beads collapse at the bottom. Now it becomes clear that the run chart is a histogram plotted on a time line. You might think of it the other way: A run chart is a stretched-out histogram. If the commute time run chart were rotated 90 degrees, it would look like the illustration.

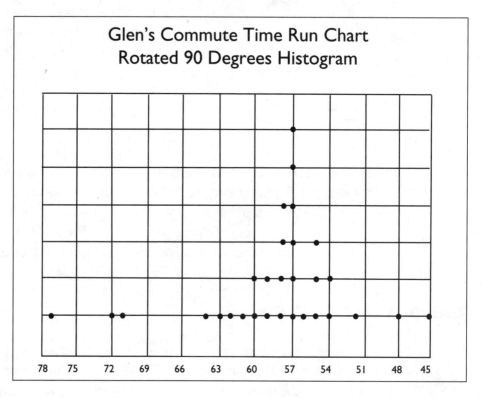

This flexible way of thinking about data is a reminder that data is merely a window into a much larger pool of numbers. Just as you must sometimes look out of different windows to begin to get a clear view, you may have to use different tools to get different views using the same data. Some recurring patterns and possible reasons for them will come clear only when you try looking at the data in different ways.

Make a histogram of your travel times. Do you see a special pattern in the times you recorded? After you have identified several possible patterns derived from the same data, you may want to brainstorm some things you might do to improve your process on the basis of data.

Two of the most common ways to enhance a process are to reduce the variation or to improve the average.

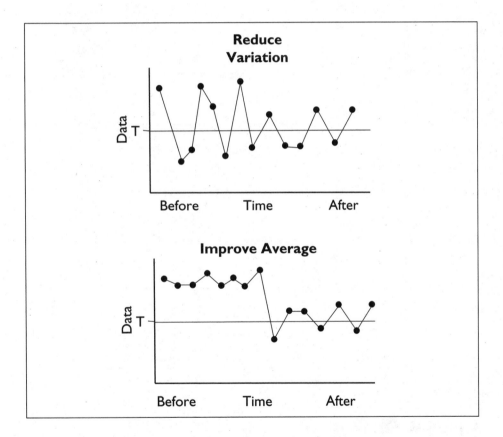

Your measurement system should yield the information you need to solve problems and improve processes so you can control future results.

When using a run chart, remember these key signals:

▶ Seven data points in a row steadily rise or fall.

▶ Seven data points in a row are on one or the other side of the average.

▶ One data point causes a spike in the line.

In addition, when one data point is beyond the customer's specification value, you'll know there is a problem. We will show you how to display the specification value and something called the control limits in the next chapter. For now, the easy-to-remember rule is 7–7–1.

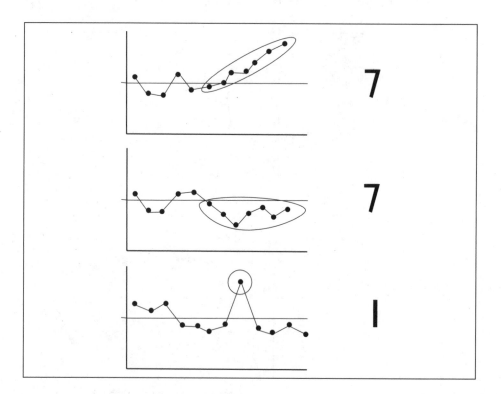

Just for Fun

Ed is back! He's going to give you another chance. You need to get to the end of the circular path from the beginning. You must walk around every one of the six circles. You cannot take any part of the route twice, but you may arrive at the same point more than once on your travels. How many different routes can you take?

If you would like to check your answer, our solution is in Appendix B.

5

Judgment

When to Take Action and When to Leave Things Alone

Introduction

Things change over time, and measurement reveals those changes. Merely drawing a picture of variation and change is not enough. You need to plot what is happening to your process. Run charts plot changes over time. One great dilemma is knowing when to take action and when to leave things alone. A powerful method for deciding whether or not to change is a process called control charting. This chapter introduces control charting, sometimes known as statistical process control.

Charting has been used successfully in tens of thousands of applications. Every control chart is different, but they all follow mathematical rules. The middle portion of this chapter contains detailed, step-by-step instructions for constructing a control chart. The math is not that difficult. In fact, it is just simple arithmetic—addition, subtraction, multiplication, and division. The calculations are not the important part of charting. It does not matter whether you use paper and pencil, a calculator, or a computer. The power of charting lies in your ability to use this tool to understand better why things are as they are and how you can improve them. As with most tools, the benefit is in the use. A hammer is useful only if you pick it up and drive a nail with it.

The chapter ends with some tips on using control charts. You may want to read this chapter more than once. It takes most people a while to absorb the concepts and benefits of charting.

What Is Good and What Is Bad

This chapter is a long one. You'll need to hold onto your seat because you will have to do some arithmetic, and things may get a little confusing. Please feel free to use a calculator or a computer. We are not trying to teach you how to do the arithmetic—only how to use numbers to make better decisions. Statistical thinking is more powerful than statistical calculations.

When you say something is good or bad, you make a value judgment in some context that has meaning for you. The notions of good and bad are significant in relation to some requirements. Numbers help you to evaluate your service or products—judge them good or bad—in relation to your customer's or your organization's needs.

A **control chart** provides a picture of the way your process is performing. It is a graphical chart with control limits and plotted values that are a statistical measure for a series of samples of the output of your process. A solid line shows the mean or average of your output.

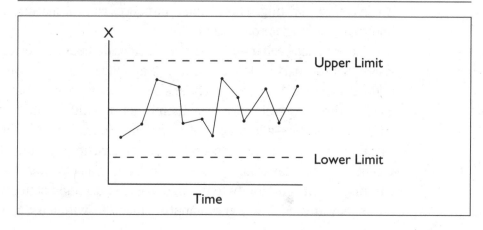

Control Chart Terms

The following are some basic terms that will help you understand what control charts are trying to tell you.

An **assignable cause** is something that contributes to the variations in your process that can be identified and tracked.

It is possible to detect assignable causes by statistical methods. By identifying and removing assignable causes, you can make your process more efficient.

Control limits provide criteria for action based on judging the significance of variations from sample to sample.

A control chart usually shows two limits, the upper limit and the lower limit, or the upper control limit (UCL) and lower control limit (LCL). We will describe each of these.

The **upper and lower limits** are generated statistically and show how your process is working. We don't normally see data above the upper limit or below the lower limit.

When statisticians developed the concept of the limit, they had to find a way to calculate it. The upper limit was defined as the average plus some padding or buffer. If the padding or buffer were very generous, values beyond the upper or lower limit would be extremely rare. If this were the case, you would tend to leave your process alone. If the pad or buffer were too small, you would violate the limit frequently, and overadjustment would result.

Statisticians decided to use 3 standard deviations as the magnitude of the padding around the mean ($\bar{x}$). This amount of padding results in values beyond the limits three times out of a thousand because of normal chance variation. These limits have proven practical for all kinds of processes all over the world. It makes the problem of over- and underadjusting manageable.

But here's a word of caution: You cannot avoid making mistakes in life. If you fail to adjust your process when it needs adjustment, then you are guilty of not fixing something that is broken. If you adjust too frequently, you are guilty of overcontrolling something that is essentially functional. Beginning drivers provide a simple analogy: They tend to oversteer until they get the feel of the road.

Control charts help you get the feel of your process. They tell you when to change things and when to leave things alone. Individual observations ideally should fall within the limits of your customer's requirements. The upper and lower limits are generated statistically and show how your process is working.

A process that is in **statistical control** has no assignable causes of variation.

A **common cause** is part of the random variation that is present within every process or system.

You can eliminate common causes only by changing the process or the system that produces them.

In an **out-of-control process,** the data points fall beyond the upper or lower control limits. Assignable causes are present.

Such a process is not in statistical control. It is not repeatable or predictable.

How to Build a Control Chart

Appendix A provides a cookbook for constructing a control chart. This cookbook was originally adapted from the *Statistical Quality Control Handbook* developed at Western Electric Company a number of years ago. It provides step-by-step directions.

If you would like to know why control charts appear as they do or how to calculate the most common control chart, look in Appendix A. The most-used control chart is called an X bar and R chart. It shows you $\overline{x}$ ($\overline{x}$ is the average) and R (R is the range).

Using a computer or a calculator makes control chart calculations very easy. However, we are firm believers in the three-P method of control charting: paper, pencil, and pocket calculator. You should do a number of control charts using the three-P method to get a sense of what the limits are, where they come from, and what they are telling you. After you understand the value of control charts, feel free to use a computer to complete them. There are many excellent software packages on the market that allow you to proceed by simply entering the data. Some computers even connect to measuring devices and automatically enter data for you.

Blank Control Chart Paper

Product _____ Process _____

Operator _____ Unit of Measure _____

Date			
Time			
Sample Measurements	1		
	2		
	3	Data	
	4		
	5		
Sum			
Average			
Range			

1	2	3	4	5	6	7	8	9	10	11	12	13	14	15	16	17	18	19	20	21	22	23	24	25

Averages

Graphs

| 1 | 2 | 3 | 4 | 5 | 6 | 7 | 8 | 9 | | 6 | 17 | 18 | 19 | 20 | 21 | 22 | 23 | 24 | 25 |

Ranges

Control charts are normally constructed on special paper that looks strange at first glance. The illustration shows a blank control chart. You will notice that it has two parts, a top part for recording data and a bottom part with two graphs. The graph portion is designed to highlight the two characteristics of data we discussed earlier, accuracy and precision. Accuracy, if you recall, is the degree to which a process is on the target. You can easily understand this characteristic by comparing the center line or average to your target. Precision is reflected in the plot of ranges on the bottom graph.

Control chart limits need not be calculated very often. Once limits have been established, weeks and months may pass before they need to be recalculated. Using a calculator or computer program makes this task quick and easy.

Using a control chart is easier than setting it up. Ideally, the people who will actually use the control chart should be able to calculate and set it up. If you can use a VCR or set a microwave, you ought to be able to calculate the limits of a control chart.

Sample Control Chart

To help you understand the symbols and the method for control chart calculations, we will take you through a sample set of calculations from beginning to end.

Kristi Smith has taken up bowling. She wants to see what kind of pattern, if any, there is in the way she bowls. She has kept track of her scores for the first 10 weeks. Because mathematicians like symbols, the number of weeks that she has bowled is the number of samples. The number of readings in a given sample is called n. Every Tuesday night, Kristi bowls four games. Therefore, n equals 4.

Step 1. Find the sum of each of Kristi's weekly bowling scores.
Adding 103, 99, 102, and 102, we get a total of 406 points scored during the week of 5/1. At the end of the first night, Kristi totals her scores for all four games. This is the sum, which she records on her control chart. In other words, she gets the sum for the week 5/1 by adding:

103
 99
102
<u>102</u>
Σ 406

She then finds the sum for the other nine nights.

Step 2. Find $\bar{x}$ for each night's bowling score.
Remember, bar means average. The letter X stands for the numbers themselves. So 406 is the sum of her bowling scores for the night of 5/1. To find her average (or X with a bar over it), Kristi must divide 406 by 4:
$406 \div 4 = 101.5$
She then calculates $\bar{x}$ for the other nine nights.

Step 3. Find the mean of all the sample averages: $\bar{\bar{x}}$.
To find the mean, you must add up the averages for all the weeks. Adding her weekly averages, Kristi arrives at a total of 971. That is the sum of the sample averages. Now divide by K, which is the number of samples. In this case, you have 10 samples; therefore, K $=$ 10. It looks like this:

Sample Averages (means)

101.50
101.00
 92.25
100.00
 95.75
 91.25
 99.00
 95.75
 99.25
<u>+ 95.50</u>
971.25

$\bar{\bar{x}}$ = mean of sample means = $971.25 \div 10 = 97.125$

Kristi's control chart is beginning to take shape. What she has done so far is reflected in the illustration.

Kristi's Bowling Scores—Control Chart
Data Record, Sums, and $\overline{X}$

Product ___Fun___   Process ___Bowling___

Operator ___Kristi Smith___   Unit of Measure ___Pins___

Date	Month/Week	5/1	5/2	5/3	5/4	6/1	6/2	6/3	6/4	7/1	7/2						
Time																	
Sample Measurements	1	103	98	94	106	104	89	101	95	98	99						
	2	99	95	94	100	93	90	99	94	99	95	} Data					
	3	102	105	93	98	92	92	98	95	100	94						
	4	102	106	100	96	90	90	98	95	100	94						
	5																
Sum Σ		406	404	381	400	379	361	396	379	397	382	$\Sigma\overline{X}$ = 971.25					
Average $\overline{X}$		101.5	101	92.25	100	94.75	90.25	99	94.75	99.25	95.5	$\overline{\overline{X}}$ mean = 97.125					

Step 4. Find the range or the spread for each of Kristi's weekly bowling evenings.

For example, in week 5/1, Kristi bowled 103, 99, 102, and 102. The highest score was 103; the lowest was 99. She found the spread or range within that sample by subtracting 99 from 103. In week 5/2, the range was 11. The calculation continued the same way for all 10 weeks.

```
 103
−99
  4
```

Step 5. Find the average of the ranges, or $\overline{R}$.

Just add up all of the ranges and divide the sum by the number of weeks, as shown.

Sample Ranges
$$
\begin{array}{c}
4 \\
11 \\
7 \\
10 \\
14 \\
3 \\
3 \\
1 \\
2 \\
\underline{5} \\
60
\end{array}
$$

$\overline{R} = 60 \div 10 = 6 = $ Mean of sample ranges

We've updated Kristi's control chart to add the range values we just calculated.

Kristi's Bowling Scores—Control Chart
Range and $\overline{R}$

Product: Fun   Process: Bowling
Operator: Kristi Smith   Unit of Measure: Pins

Date	Month Week	5/1	5/2	5/3	5/4	6/1	6/2	6/3	6/4	7/1	7/2						
Time																	
Sample Measurements	1	103	98	94	106	104	89	101	95	98	99						
	2	99	95	94	100	93	90	99	94	99	95		Data				
	3	102	105	93	98	92	92	98	95	100	94						
	4	102	106	100	96	90	90	98	95	100	94						
	5																
Sum Σ		406	404	381	400	379	361	396	379	397	382						
Average		101.5	101	92.25	100	94.75	90.25	99	94.75	99.25	95.5	$\overline{\overline{x}}$ mean = 97.125					
Range		4	11	7	10	14	3	3	1	2	5	$\overline{R} = 6$					

Step 6. Look up relationship values.

Kristi's average for her 10 weeks of bowling is 97.125. At this point, if someone asked Kristi what kind of bowler she is, Kristi could respond that on average she bowls 97.125. About half the time she bowls a little better than that; half the time she does a little worse.

The goal of control charting is to put some limits on a process and see how much variation the process exhibits. Most processes have some built-in variability. Let's apply this concept to Kristi's bowling. To take the 97.125 and put a pad or buffer around it, use the concept of the normal curve. Instead of calculating 3 standard deviations, a simpler method is to use a table and some constant factors that show the relationships between the sample size, the standard deviations, and the sample ranges. These relationships are called A_2, D_4, and D_3. They can be found in the table below and in Appendix A.

N	2	3	4	5	6	7	8	9	10
D_4	3.27	2.57	2.28	2.11	2.00	1.92	1.86	1.82	1.78
D_3	0.00	0.00	0.00	0.00	0.00	0.08	0.14	0.18	0.22
A_2	1.88	1.02	0.73	0.58	0.48	0.42	0.37	0.34	0.31
d_2	1.13	1.69	2.06	2.33	2.53	2.70	2.85	2.97	3.08

Kristi's Numbers From Table if N = 4

$$A_2 = .73$$
$$D_4 = 2.28$$
$$D_3 = 0$$

Step 7. Calculate the limits for the sample average.

Now let's plug in the equation for the upper and lower control limits. The equation may look a little intimidating, so we will describe it and then write it out. First, find the average of the sample averages (97.1), then add to it a pad or buffer (.73 times 6). Six is the average of all the ranges. In mathematics, multiplication always comes before addition. Multiply .73 by 6, and add the result to 97.1. This gives you 101.5 as the upper control limit for Kristi's bowling.

$$A_2 \times \bar{R} = .73 \times 6 = 4.38$$
$$UCL_{\bar{x}} = 97.1 + 4.38 = 101.48$$
$$LCL_{\bar{x}} = 97.1 - 4.38 = 92.72$$

In other words, if Kristi averages higher than 101 on any night, then her game is significantly different—better than what it used to be. On the other hand, if her average for the evening's four games is below 92.7, then she has done something bad to her game. When values occur outside the limits, the evidence indicates that statistically something has occurred, but the chart gives no indication what has occurred. The answer lies outside the control chart. The answer as to why the values are the way they are lies within the system that developed the data. Perhaps Kristi forgot her bowling shoes, or she was not feeling well, or she was distracted by bowlers in other lanes. The answer came from understanding the system, not in the numbers.

The control chart of the sample averages shows how stable the process is relative to its mean.

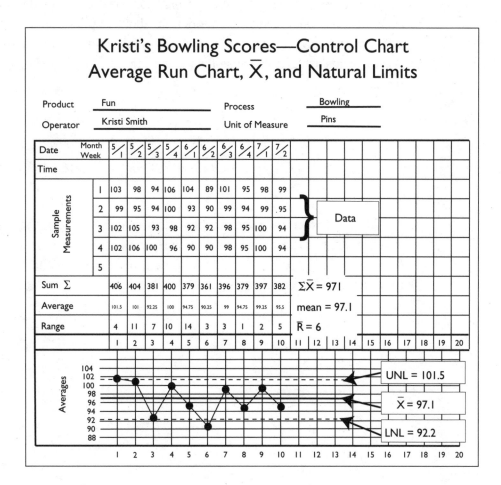

Kristi's Bowling Scores—Control Chart
Average Run Chart, $\bar{X}$, and Natural Limits

| Product | Fun | | Process | Bowling |
| Operator | Kristi Smith | | Unit of Measure | Pins |

Step 8. Calculate the limit for the range.

The next step is to calculate the limits of the variation in the games themselves. How much variation should Kristi normally exhibit in a given evening? Here you use the mathematical constants D_4 and D_3 to give you upper and lower limits of the variation in her game. In other words, measure variation. Note: There are two graphs on our control chart. The graph of the ranges measures the precision or the repeatability of the process.

Again, we will describe the equation before writing it out. The upper control limit is D_4 times $\bar{R}$. For Kristi's example, D_4 is the mathematical constant, 2.28, which we found in the table on page 70. When you multiply this number by the average range of $\bar{R}$, 6, the result is 13.68.

Remember, 6 was the average range for Kristi's games. On any given evening, she should never vary more than about 14 pins from her best game to her worst game. If her scores vary by more than 14 pins, it shows that there is some assignable cause for the variation in the way she bowled that night.

$$UCL_R = D_4 \times \bar{R} = 2.28 \times 6 = 13.68$$

$$LCL_R = D_3 \times \bar{R} = 0.00 \times 6 = 00.00$$

After you complete the mathematical calculations for the upper and lower limits, you draw the boundary lines on the bottom of the graph paper. It is best to only use approximately 75 percent of the available space on the range chart. This leaves room to plot large values.

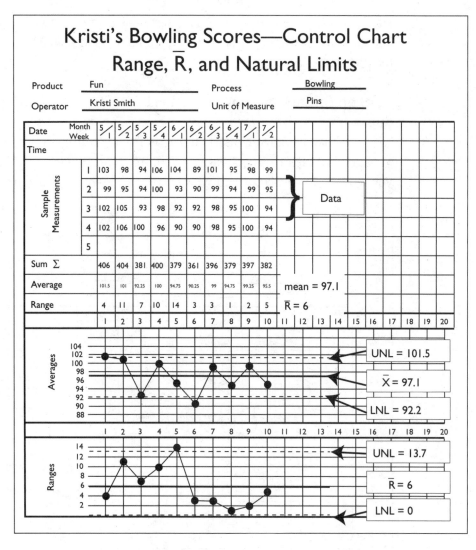

Kristi's Bowling Scores—Control Chart
Range, $\bar{R}$, and Natural Limits

| Product | Fun | | Process | Bowling |
| Operator | Kristi Smith | | Unit of Measure | Pins |

Date	Month / Week	5/1	5/2	5/3	5/4	6/1	6/2	6/3	6/4	7/1	7/2									
Time																				
Sample Measurements	1	103	98	94	106	104	89	101	95	98	99									
	2	99	95	94	100	93	90	99	94	99	95									
	3	102	105	93	98	92	92	98	95	100	94									
	4	102	106	100	96	90	90	98	95	100	94									
	5																			
Sum Σ		406	404	381	400	379	361	396	379	397	382									
Average		101.5	101	92.25	100	94.75	90.25	99	94.75	99.25	95.5	mean = 97.1								
Range		4	11	7	10	14	3	3	1	2	5	$\bar{R}$ = 6								

Data

UNL = 101.5

$\bar{X}$ = 97.1

LNL = 92.2

UNL = 13.7

$\bar{R}$ = 6

LNL = 0

Scaling can be an important part of the control charting. Scales that are too wide can make the data look erratic. They make you think there is variation that requires action when in fact the variation is just natural or normal. Remember, the goal of control charting is to understand what variations are most likely due to chance and what variations are due to something special that has happened. Statistical purists say plot the ranges first to see if indeed you have a stable process that is repeatable over time. If the process is not stable, it is not a single process but a series of different processes with different standard deviations. Use a run chart, not a control chart to study unstable processes.

Step 9. Study the control chart and identify patterns associated with causes.

Now that we have constructed Kristi's bowling control chart, we ask, What does it mean? When reading a control chart, remember that it will tell you when to make changes in your process and when to leave it alone.

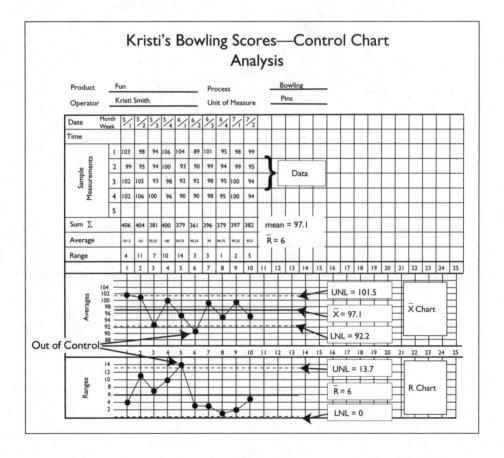

Kristi's bowling game might give us cause for concern. It has not leveled yet. The first week in June she exhibited a range or variation of 14. This means her process that week was not part of her normal way of bowling. Something unusual happened that particular week. If Kristi understands what happened and she is at peace with it, she may want to view that week's scores as normal scores.

Kristi might want to continue bowling for a while until her scores level out. When they do, she should recalculate the control limits on what she calls normal operating conditions. If you look at the averages in the range chart, you will see they vary within the upper and lower natural limits except for the second week in June (6/2). Perhaps what happened the first week in June caused Kristi to change her game somehow. In the second week of June, her games were very constant. Although her bowling was pretty bad that night, it showed little variation. Only Kristi herself or someone who understands bowling could interpret the data in terms of what it means in real life. The calculations merely give a frame of reference for that interpretation.

The goal in most processes is to reduce variation and drive to the target. The goal for Kristi would be to average 300 every night, with no variation in any game. That is an ideal—something for her to work toward. Good luck! The control chart will help her understand the extent to which her variation is improving or declining. That is, the control chart can help her understand how her average is moving toward or away from her goal.

There are many other kinds of control charts and literally hundreds of different ways to configure control chart paper to meet specific needs. Appendix A will tell you more about control charts.

A point where data falls beyond the control limits is not the only indication that your process needs attention. As you will see later in the chapter, there are many data patterns that indicate possible trouble spots. It is important to be on the lookout for these patterns as well as for points beyond the limits. It is also important to control chart your process after changes have been made. This will help you to determine if your process is in control. Once a process is in control, only changes in the system will improve it.

A goal of using control charts is to make uniform products or deliver consistent services over time. A control chart shows when something new or different is affecting the process. It also shows when the variation in what you do increases or decreases. However, bringing a process into mathematical or statistical control is not enough to meet your customer's needs. It is possible to produce a product or service that is statistically in control and still lose your customer. Why is this so? Because the statistical limits that you have calculated have nothing to do with your customer's upper and lower specification limits. What your customer wants from your process and the capabilities of your process may be significantly different. Specification limits are determined by the use to which the customer puts the product or service, not the method you use to produce the product or service. You must compare the variation inherent in your process with the variation that your customer wants.

More often than not, the 7–7–1 rule for run charts is sufficient to let us optimize the data available from a control chart. Putting next to the control chart an action plan with specific actions defined by participants in the process allows you to come up with a uniform response. For example, if you are measuring salt content in potato chips and you get seven samples in a row trending upward, you need to check to make sure that the salt-filling operation is not going berserk.

Control in Relation to Specifications

The casebook below shows the four possible cases that any process can exhibit in relation to control and specifications. Each of the four states is shown by a control chart combined with a histogram. The control chart shows how the process is performing over time, and the histogram shows how well the process is meeting the customer's needs. USL and LSL refer to the upper and lower specification limits demanded by the customer. UNL and LNL refer to the upper and lower natural limits that are inherent in the way the process is working; those limits may or may not produce satisfactory results. It is important to pay attention to both sets of measurements. Natural limits are the ends of the product distribution—the mean plus and minus 3 standard deviations.

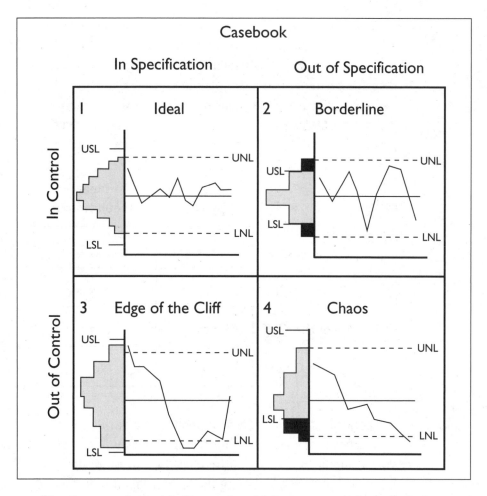

The first case is the ideal state, in which a process is in statistical control as shown by a control chart. The variation of the process is between the natural upper and lower limits. The histogram of the product distribution is a normal curve, showing that the customer's needs are met. Over 99 percent of the product or service falls within specifications. This ideal state is temporary. If left to their own devices, processes break, decay, and become less efficient.

The second case is the borderline state. A borderline process is in statistical control. However, it is producing some product that does not meet the customer's requirements. This process would meet the customer's requirements if you reduced the variation. (You could also sort the product to meet your customer's needs, although that approach is not efficient.)

The third case is the edge-of-the-cliff state, in which the process is out of statistical control, wandering beyond the natural limits. Because the limits of the customer's specifications are broader than the natural limits of the process, the customer is not complaining—yet.

The final case is the chaos state. Things are in chaos when what you do is not repeatable. Your results are scattered. They are not in control, and the product or service does not meet your customer's requirements.

	Consistent over Time	Meet Requirements	Results
1. Ideal	Yes	Yes	😃
2. Borderline	Yes	No	😐
3. Edge of the Cliff	No	Yes	😐
4. Chaos	No	No	☹️

Control charts allow you to look at the variation of your product over time in terms of statistical pattern, repeatability, and your success in meeting your customer's needs. Control charts incorporate many different types of numerical patterns, including the histogram and the run chart. Do not use a control chart if some simpler tool will work. Do not use a simpler tool if you need the information a control chart can give you.

The concept of natural limits can get a bit crazy. Natural limits are the form the process takes, given current configurations of resources and operating conditions. Natural limits of plus or minus 3σ encompass most of what you do. However, when the sample size is 2, 3, 4, 5, 6, or greater, you must calculate the spread or variation in the process using table values. The upper and lower control limits on control charts are indicators of the extremes of sample mean variation, not individual variation. Therefore, it is not appropriate to put upper and lower specification limits on X bar and R charts. On those charts, you are comparing individual readings to average readings.

Typically, you want the upper and lower specification limits much broader than the natural limits of the process. The broader the specifications, the easier they are to meet.

Using control charts wisely can improve your judgment, your processes, your results, and your bottom line. To make appropriate changes, you should exercise good judgment based on data. However, you may face a dilemma in deciding whether or not to make an adjustment. Correcting one error often introduces another error. You have a choice of two actions: You can leave all the settings as they are, or you can adjust them. If something has changed and you do not adjust your process, you are making a mistake. On the other hand, if you adjust the process when adjustment is not called for, you will ruin the new output. If you use the 3-standard-deviation logic of control charts, you can reduce uncalled-for adjustments. The good news is that unneeded adjustments will occur less than 1 percent of the time.

Decision Table

Fact \ Act	Adjust	Do Not Adjust
Process Changed	OK	Error
Process Not Changed	Error	OK

There are advantages and disadvantages in maximizing or minimizing each kind of error, overadjusting and underadjusting. The decision maker's dilemma is that it is impossible to minimize both kinds of errors. By minimizing one error, you maximize the other. Using statistical patterns such as those from control charts helps you balance the two kinds of errors. Known statistical patterns enable you to minimize both errors relative to each other.

Process capability indices, a special measure designed to compare requirements to performance, are a helpful adjunct to control charts. Chapter 6 will deal with process capability indices.

The use of control charts must start with leadership, not with the workers. Leadership takes a major step forward when they stop asking for explanations of random variation.

W. Edwards Deming

When making decisions, it is important to show good judgment. Your judgment can improve if you know what your natural limits are and how well your process is working in relation to those limits.

When you say something is good or bad, you make a value judgment in some context that has meaning for you. Numbers help you evaluate your product or service in relation to your customer's needs. Control charts can help you understand your limits and how well your process is working. A control chart

▶ Helps create a graphical picture of the performance of your process,

▶ Identifies things that are not a normal part of your process,

▶ Lets you see how your process is performing currently,

▶ Shows if your process is performing within its natural limits,

▶ Does not work on processes that are not clearly identified, and

▶ Must be analyzed.

The oft-heard excuse "I changed it because the control chart told me to" is not valid. The control chart can only indicate how your process is working in relation to its limits.

The 7–7–1 Rule

Significant Change 1. Seven data points in a row steadily rising or falling need to be investigated.

Significant Change 2. Seven data points in a row on one side of the average need to be investigated.

Significant Change 3. One data point outside of the UNL or LNL needs to be investigated.

Control Chart Terms

N   The number of the sample size

R   Range—the difference between the largest and the smallest in a given sample

$\overline{R}$	The average of the Rs of the samples. A bar means to add the numbers and divide the sum by the number of numbers (average).
UCL	Upper control limit—3σ above the center line or R bar. The upper natural limit is the point beyond which data normally does not appear.
LCL	Lower control limit—3σ below the center line
$\overline{x}$	Average or middle
$\overline{\overline{x}}$	The average of all the sample averages
Σ	"The sum of"
CL	The center line of the control chart; either $\overline{x}$ or $\overline{R}$

Just for Fun

Billy the Balladeer Bullfrog has been serenading his sweetheart, Mildred. She was sitting on the edge of a 10-foot-deep well. Unfortunately, she has fallen to the bottom of the well. She is able to jump up 2 feet every hour on the hour, but she slips down 1 foot every hour on the half hour. How long will Billy have to sing before Mildred frees herself from the well?

The solution can be found in Appendix B.

6

Usefulness

How Well Your Process Meets Your Customer's Needs

Introduction

Most things in life are not good or bad by themselves. Good or bad is relative to some frame of reference. Is 105°F good or bad? If you are painting your house and the outdoor temperature is 105°F, that's bad. If you are in a sauna at the gym, 105°F is good. Process variation must be compared with what is desired. Requirements are determined by your customers and how they use what you provide them. To state it simply, compare what you "got" with what you "want." This comparison is called process capability. A comical example involving driving a car across a bridge will be used in this chapter to create a visual picture of requirements versus performance. Requirements are what we "want"; performance is what we "get." This chapter develops a measure of "wants" and "gots." The measure is called Cp and its big brother is called CpK. As usual, the math is less important than the concept, but often we learn the concept by doing the math.

Process Capability

Customers may be very different. It is hard to hit a target unless you know what the target is. For instance, if you are cooking a steak for someone, the person will be much more satisfied if you cook it the way he or she likes it.

You must find out what is most important to your customers. First, you must determine who your customers are. Then you need to understand their requirements. Finally, you need to determine how well you are meeting their requirements. In other words, answer these questions:

- ▶ Who are my customers?
- ▶ What do they want?
- ▶ What are they getting?
- ▶ How do I measure what they are getting?

Today's market calls for consistency of products and services. Process capability is a good way to understand the results of all of your hard work. Process capability measures the ability of your process to meet your customer's requirements (specifications).

A **process** comprises everything that works together to produce a product or service.

A typical organization has only 8 to 12 processes. However, each person in the organization has 8 to 12 processes in his or her job. Outside of the job, each one also has another 8 to 12 processes that are important to him or her.

To visualize this concept, think about the many processes in your daily life. For instance, one process involves paying bills; another involves getting to work. Take a few minutes and list the 8 to 12 most important processes that make up your daily life.

Process capability is the ability to satisfy your internal or external customer's needs. Who is the customer in your bill-paying process? The customer is the company you are paying. That process entails many steps, such as earning money, writing a check, and mailing the payment. Your process capability index would measure the extent to which you paid your bills on time.

Process capability rates the ability of your system to meet your customer's need. It is a statistical measure of the relationship between variations in your process and the specification. You cannot determine process capability until the process is stable.

Cp Ratio

By applying a few formulas, you can easily tell whether your process is capable of meeting specifications.

This is a sample of the text for the definition, or these are more synonyms and usages that are commonly found in the English language.

Process capability (Cp) compares what you are currently doing with what your customer wants.

A histogram shows what you are doing. Your customer's wants are your goal posts. You need to kick the ball between the goal posts.

If the variation within your process—what you do—is less than the variation in what the customer wants, your Cp index is greater than one. The larger the Cp index, the better off you are. If the Cp of your process is equal to one, the variation of your process is the same as your customer's specifications. On the average, your process will produce something unacceptable to the customer about three times out of a thousand. If the Cp index of your process is less than one, your process is unable to meet the customer's requirements. Not meeting the customer's need is a bad thing.

Process Capability (Cp) Equation

$$Cp = \frac{USL - LSL}{6\sigma}$$

The process capability index is the ratio of the spread in a process (allowed by the specification limits) to the actual amount of variation in the process. You can use a simple equation to calculate Cp.

The upper and lower specification limits are what the customer wants—in other words, how much variation the customer can tolerate. Your current level of variation is what your customer receives. It is what you do or produce. As you recall, the measure of variation is the standard deviation, or σ. The 6σ measure includes 99.7 percent of what you do. Divide what you do into what the customer wants. Start with the upper specification limit (USL) and subtract the lower specification limit (LSL). Divide the result of the difference by 6σ. The resulting total is the process capability, or Cp.

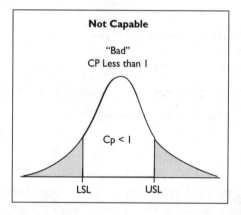

Water Test Example

$$Cp = \frac{10\ ml - 6\ ml}{6\ (1\ ml)} = \frac{4\ ml}{6\ ml} = 0.67$$

Not Capable

"Bad"
CP Less than 1

Cp < 1

LSL   USL

Here is an example involving a water testing process. The specification for the process is 6 ml (milliliters) to 10 ml; the standard deviation is 1 ml. The Cp index is 0.67.

A process with a capability index less than one is not capable of meeting specifications. The spread of the distribution is a greater amount of variability than the specifications will allow. The customer will consistently be receiving out-of-specification service or product. To stop delivering bad service or product, you will need to put in place an extensive and expensive inspection system.

To make that abstract concept more concrete, here is an example from the experience of one of the authors and his wife. They were moving to a new home in the country. There were two ways to the house; however, the shortest way crossed an old wooden bridge like the one in the illustration.

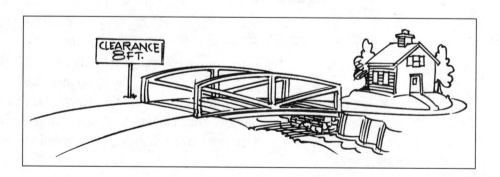

CLEARANCE
8 FT.

$$CP = \frac{Want}{Have} = \frac{Bridge}{Truck} = \frac{8\,feet}{12\,feet} = .67$$

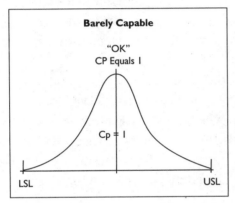

The author was riding his motorcycle, his wife was driving the car, and a moving company employee was driving the moving van. The moving van was 12 feet wide. When it reached the bridge, it was unable to cross because the Cp was less than one. The Cp ratio told them their process could not meet their requirements. They had to adjust the process by having the truck take the long way around and go the extra 10 miles.

A process with a Cp ratio equal to one is just barely capable of meeting the customer's specifications. Three times out of a thousand, it will not meet your customer's requirements. Would you like to fly an airline that lands safely 997 times out of 1,000, or would you prefer a Cp ratio that is larger than one? Most people complain loudly about many processes that are just barely capable of meeting needs. They do so knowing that there may be a process problem. Who wants to be in the 3 planes out of 1,000 that crash?

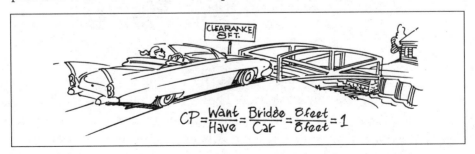

$$CP = \frac{Want}{Have} = \frac{Bridge}{Car} = \frac{8\,feet}{8\,feet} = 1$$

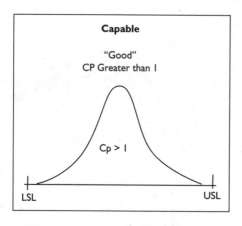

Capable

"Good"
CP Greater than 1

Cp > 1

LSL   USL

Let's go back to our moving day problem. The car driven by the author's wife was 8 feet wide; the bridge was also 8 feet wide. Did the author's wife also have to drive the extra 10 miles? She did not, but it was a very tight squeeze through the bridge. In this case, the Cp was equal to one; this indicates that the process was capable but there was no room for variation. A car that was any wider could not have crossed the bridge.

The best situation is a process capability ratio greater than one. In this case, the variability in the process is less than the variability allowed by the specifications. Instances in which the process produces something defective will be extremely rare. This is the type of ratio we depend on where critical components are concerned and when safety or security is at stake. Processes that have a large Cp ratio should be your goal. A way to remember this is "Big is best."

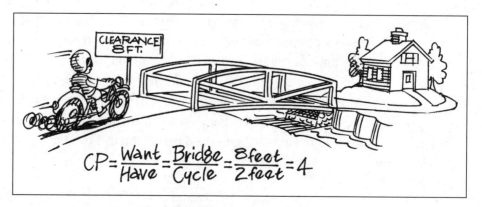

$$CP = \frac{Want}{Have} = \frac{Bridge}{Cycle} = \frac{8 feet}{2 feet} = 4$$

Let's apply this concept to the moving day example. The author's motorcycle was only 2 feet wide. The Cp was greater than one. This tells us the process had great potential to meet the requirement of the motorcycle's crossing the bridge. In fact, it could still get over the bridge if unexpected variations

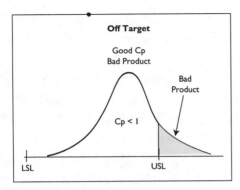

occurred, such as a dog coming in the opposite direction. The author on his motorcycle could zigzag across the bridge with room to spare.

Although the Cp ratio is a powerful measure of process consistency, it has limitations. It only indicates the potential of a process to meet the specifications. It is not a measure of how much of the product actually falls within specifications. A process that is centered near either of the specification limits can yield a large amount of bad product, even with an excellent Cp ratio. Many customers now require the use of the Cpk ratio to ensure the uniformity of products or services that they receive.

The author could still run his cycle off of the bridge if he were not paying attention, even though the bridge left plenty of room.

Cpk Ratio

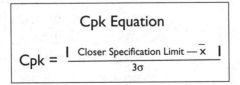

The Cpk ratio equals the Cp ratio when the process is centered on the specifications. When the process is not centered, the Cpk will be smaller than the Cp. The Cpk ratio is also very simple. It uses the USL or the LSL, depending on which is closer to center of the curve.

The Cpk ratio can help you predict the percentage of nonconforming product your process will yield. For example, a Cpk ratio of 0.5 is associated with 6.7 percent out-of-specification product. A 1.33 Cpk results in .003 percent nonconforming product, and a 2.0 Cpk is linked to a defect rate of 0.0000001 percent, or one defective item per billion.

Many companies think that a 2.0 Cpk is an ideal rate. This may be true if you are producing billions of items. However, if you are producing a small volume of high-value items, it may be more cost-effective for you to sort and inspect your product rigorously. You can convert Cpk into the percentage of nonconforming product; the chart shows this conversion. These estimates apply to a single specification limit of a process that is normally distributed and in statistical control.

It may be helpful to look at an example of Cpk from a firm that ships packages. The specification is that 80 to 84 packages per day can be delayed. The mean is 83 packages per day; the standard deviation is 0.5 packages.

The process appears capable when Cp is calculated, but the Cpk index reveals that a considerable number of late packages will result.

Let's go back to our moving day situation. Remember that you want precision and accuracy. The Cp

Cpk Converted to Nonconforming Product

Cpk	Percent Nonconforming
0.40	11.5
0.50	6.7
0.60	3.6
0.70	1.8
0.80	0.82
0.90	0.35
1.00	0.14
1.10	0.05
1.20	0.02
1.30	0.005
1.33	0.003
1.50	0.0003
1.60	0.0001
1.67	0.00003
2.00	0.000001%

Late Packages

$$Cp = \frac{84\ pk - 80\ pk}{6\ (0.5\ pk)} = \frac{4\ pk}{3\ pk} = 1.33$$

$$Cpk = \frac{84\ pk - 83\ pk}{3\ (0.5\ pk)} = \frac{1\ pk}{1.5\ pk} = 0.67$$

ratio helped us understand precision. If you remember, the car had a Cp ratio of exactly one. If the car were to cross the bridge, it had to be very accurate. However, let's look at the motorcycle's Cpk. The Cp greater than 1 tells us that the process (the 2-foot-wide motorcycle) had the potential to meet the requirements (the 8-foot-wide bridge). The Cpk greater than 1 also tells us that the process does meet the requirements, that our aim is accurate.

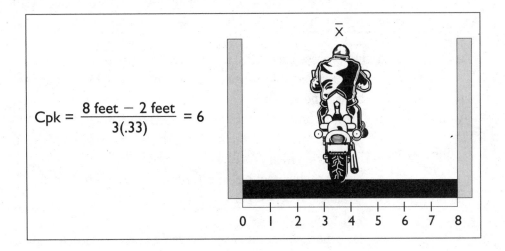

$$\text{Cpk} = \frac{8 \text{ feet} - 2 \text{ feet}}{3(.33)} = 6$$

Both indices are used to measure process capability. The Cp index measures the precision of the process. The Cpk index measures both the accuracy and the precision of the process. Both indices allow you to

- ▶ Concentrate technical know-how and other resources on processes with low Cp's and Cpk's,
- ▶ Track improvement in the performance of your process over time, and
- ▶ Improve your aim at your goal post.

Using Cp and Cpk

The larger the value of Cp and Cpk, the better off you are. The larger those values are, the more likely you are to be able to meet your customer's requirements. **Tip:** Complete a process capability study only after the process is stable. Cp assumes that variable data has been generated, that the process is distributed normally, and that the process is centered on the customer's specifications.

> Cp and Cpk can be used to prevent defects by taking action on the process rather than having to take action on the output. Sorting and rework of output are expensive actions. It is usually more efficient and effective to fix the process. It is better to quit producing bad products and services than to rely on sorting and fixing customer complaints.

Using process capability indices enables you to
▶ Determine which processes are not capable of meeting your customer's needs,
▶ Identify processes that are not operating at maximum efficiency,
▶ Identify the processes that have the least margin of capability,
▶ Prioritize which processes to improve first,
▶ Estimate the amount of your output that will be bad, and
▶ Evaluate process performance over extended periods to maintain your best practices.

Today's markets require ever-increasing proof of quality and consistency of products and services. Process capability is one tool often used to communicate the amount of variability in processes. Several indices of process capability are available. The two most commonly used are the Cp and Cpk indices. Use the one that is most appropriate for you.

Just for Fun

Laura is getting ready to make some jelly. Unfortunately, she has lost her measuring cups. All she has are two jars. Her countertops are covered with berries, so she cannot store anything there. Laura knows that one jar holds 9 cups and the other jar holds 4 cups. Her recipe calls for 6 cups of sugar. How can she measure 6 cups of sugar with only the two jars she has available?

Our answer is in Appendix B.

7 Experimentation

Finding New Insights

Introduction

Where do better ideas and methods come from? Every so often, someone has to take a chance and try something new. How did we learn that potatoes are good to eat and rocks are not? Someone took a chance and tried to eat a rock. The attempt seemed like a failure. It *was* a failure in terms of finding something edible, but it was a success in that learning occurred. Progress requires continual new learning. To learn and grow, we must experiment and try new things. It is not easy. Most people do not like to try new things; most of us resist even rearranging our furniture.

Although new insights may be the result of luck, experiments are most productive if we plan them. Waiting to trip over a new idea is much less dependable than planning an experiment, carrying it out, carefully checking the results, and then taking action based on the new learning.

This chapter gives a brief introduction to the design of experiments. We have found that working with a group of subject matter experts and listing possible new ways of performing a task is a good first step. Conducting actual experiments to test the new methods provides hard evidence as to which one is best. We will illustrate this approach with an everyday example involving pie baking. As with other measurement tools, the power lies not in the tool but in the people using it. You can't learn to ride a bike by watching someone else ride one. You have to experiment and get on.

Most of what I learn, I learn by screwing it up the first time.
NORMAN SCHWARTZKOPF

Designing Experiments

How good is good enough? This question has been asked throughout history. There are three ways of answering it.

1. Distinguish good from bad. All you have to do is sort the good

stuff from the bad stuff or reduce variation until everything is within specifications. Just as in football, when you kick the ball at the goal posts, you score when the ball goes between the posts. Those kicks that send the ball between the goal posts are good, and those that don't are bad. Applied in pie production, this approach means checking each pie to make certain it is good before selling it.

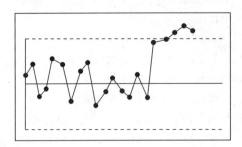

2. Control variation over time. When you identify and remove special causes of variation, you put your process under statistical control. In pie production, for example, this means having a standard, repeatable way of baking pies so that they always turn out the same.

3. Drive the process to its target. In this approach, you focus on what the process should produce and then modify it to produce exactly the desired result. For example, if a pie is sold as a 24-ounce pie, then it should in fact weigh 24 ounces. If any pie weighs more than 24 ounces, you lose money. On the other hand, pies weighing less than 24 ounces cause your customer to lose value and become upset. The goal is 24 ounces precisely, not 24 ounces plus or minus anything.

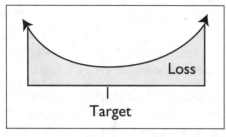

No matter which of the three ways you choose to look at your process, experiments can help you get where you need to go. When you have decided to improve your process, how will you find that better way? A well-planned experiment is just what you need. We recommend following these four steps.

1. **Plan your experiment.** When developing a plan for your experiment, you must begin by determining what outcome is important. You then need to identify what affects the outcome you are looking for.
2. **Do the experiment.** When performing the experiment, it is important to have a schedule for running it. You must also observe and record the results.
3. **Study the results.** When studying the results of your experiment, you need to look for patterns and relationships between the elements you have identified as affecting the outcome.
4. **Take action.** After you have studied the results, you need to develop a new and better way of reaching your desired results.

This four-step experiment method was first developed by Walter Shewhart and promoted by W. Edwards Deming. It is used for designing experiments as well as solving problems.

Your experiment may entail a planned design. If you involve a statistician, he or she may help you design an experiment differently than you would have in the past. The table shows some comparisons between methods of experimentation in traditional settings and in modern settings.

Comparison of Methods of Experimentation

Criterion	Traditional	Modern
Basic procedure	Hold everything constant except the factor under investigation.	Plan the experiment to evaluate several factors.
Experimental conditions	Hold material, workers, and machines constant throughout the entire experiment.	Realize difficulty of holding conditions reasonably constant throughout an entire experiment.
Experimental error	Not measured.	Measured.
Results of evaluation	Evaluate result with a consideration of the amount of experimental error.	Evaluate result by comparing result with the measure of experimental error.
Effect of sequence of experiments	Assume that sequence has no effect.	Guard against by randomization.
Effect of varying both factors simultaneously (interaction)	Not adequately planned into experiment.	Experiment can be planned to include an investigation for interaction between factors.
Validity of results	Results are misleading or erroneous if interaction exists.	Even if interaction exists, a valid evaluation of the results can be made.
Number of measurements	For valid information, more measurements are needed than in the modern approach.	Fewer measurements are needed for useful and valid information.
Definition of problem	Objective of experiment frequently is not defined clearly.	In order to design experiment, it is necessary to define the objective in detail.

To gain insights into possible better ways to run your process, you need first to decide what results you want. Let's go back to the pie example. You may decide that you can make pies more efficiently, and you consider many possible ways to improve the process—for example, changing the oven temperature, increasing or decreasing the baking time, or increasing or decreasing the moisture content in the recipe.

A well-planned experiment is tailor-made for meeting specific objectives and satisfying practical constraints. After the problem and constraints have been clearly defined, a statistician is usually engaged to help develop an experimental layout that will minimize the required effort and maximize the usefulness of the information you get from the experiment.

When designing an experiment to improve a process, you need to talk with the people involved, either individually or in a group. Find out what they think is important to their customer. Then have them describe what they do that affects that result. For example, if the customer likes the moisture content of the pies, it is important to identify the variables that might affect moisture content. Some of those variables might be oven temperature, baking time, water content prior to baking, amount of cornstarch in the recipe, thickness of crust, and so forth. It is not unusual to identify 12 to 18 variables that people think may affect the end product.

In this case, you think that temperature, baking time, and the amount of cornstarch in the pie recipe are probably the key factors that determine how moist the final product is. You then design an experiment to find out if you are correct. You make some pies with a little extra cornstarch and some with a little less cornstarch than normal. You bake some pies a little more than normal and some a little less than normal. You bake some at a little higher temperature than normal and some at a lower temperature than normal.

In all, you make nine pies. The first one is your standard pie, baked at the normal temperature of 350°F, for the normal baking time of 50 minutes, and with the normal amount of cornstarch, $\frac{1}{4}$ ($\frac{2}{8}$) cup. This pie is perfect. It weighs 184 grams. We call this perfect pie a control sample.

A **control sample** is what all of your output will be measured against.

Factor Trial	X$_1$	X$_2$	X$_3$
1	+	+	+
2	+	+	−
3	+	−	+
4	+	−	−
5	−	+	+
6	−	+	−
7	−	−	+
8	−	−	−

Wow! With nine pies and three different variable factors, you have many different pies and combinations to keep track of. The sequence table will make it easier to keep track of what factors to change and in what order. The first column in the table shows identifying numbers for the pies you are going to bake. The factors (X$_1$, X$_2$, and X$_3$) are the three things you have decided to vary: temperature, baking time, and amount of cornstarch. You hope to find a combination producing a pie that is as good as you currently bake but that you can produce more efficiently.

Pie #	Temperature	Time (minutes)	Cornstarch (cups)	Grams	Result
1	375°	55	3/8	170	Dry
2	375°	55	1/8	165	Dusty
3	375°	45	3/8	172	Crumbly
4	375°	45	1/8	184	Just right
5	325°	55	3/8	190	Soft
6	325°	55	1/8	196	Goopy
7	325°	45	3/8	199	Runny
8	325°	45	1/8	205	Soupy

Experiments by their nature can lead you to new results, but you need the liberty to learn. You must be willing to try and fail. You may find new and better ways of doing things, or you may not.

When you conduct your experiment, you will set the baking temperature sometimes at 375°F and sometimes at 325°F. Sometimes you will increase the baking time to 55 minutes; sometimes you will decrease it to 45 minutes. The amount of cornstarch, which is the third variable, will be 3/8 cup at the high end and 1/8 cup at the low end.

According to the sequence table, the first experimental pie will be prepared with extra time, extra temperature, and extra cornstarch. Therefore, it will be baked at 375°F for 55 minutes and will contain $\frac{3}{8}$ cup of cornstarch. The second experimental pie will have higher temperature, extra time, and less cornstarch. You will bake it at 375°F for 55 minutes. It will contain $\frac{1}{8}$ cup of cornstarch.

When the experimental pies are done, you and your customers try them. The first pie, which was cooked at a higher temperature, for a longer time, and with $\frac{3}{8}$ cup of cornstarch, turns out to be very dry. The last pie, cooked for a shorter time, at a lower temperature, and with less cornstarch, turns out to be soupy. The pie experiment results table shows how you baked each of the pies. It also shows the results that you found as each pie was tested.

Using a rigorous experimental method enables you to design a well-thought-out process that produces something your customer wants. The key is to identify specific customer needs and the variables that will result in the meeting of those needs. Be willing to experiment even when your process is running well. In fact, that is the best time to do so!

There are many methods of experimentation. The method you choose depends a great deal on what you want the experiment to accomplish.

Experiments usually generate an incredible amount of data—too much for you to study or interpret effectively. Using random sampling can help you reduce your data to a workable amount while retaining all of the characteristics generated by the experiment. We will talk more about random sampling in Chapter 8.

Design of experiments will be covered in greater detail in another book in this series, which will be devoted to various methods for designing better experiments.

Designing experiments is an effective and efficient way to gain insights into ways you might run your process better. A well-designed experiment can eliminate the negative effects of two or more variables while allowing you to evaluate the interactions between the variables.

Designed experiments are effective because they
▶ Are laid out to accomplish particular objectives,
▶ Help you make maximum use of minimum data, time, and dollars,

▶ Are designed to answer specific questions, and

▶ Enable you to separate variation due to planned changes from other experimental variation.

A designed experiment establishes cause-and-effect relationships between several variables and the outcomes being studied because several factors are changed at the same time in a deliberate way.

Experiments yield critical information about service and manufacturing processes. They have three main objectives.

▶ An experiment can detect differences that you can use to take action.

▶ An experiment can reveal relationships between factors.

▶ An experiment measures the effects of varying aspects of a process.

Behold the turtle: He only makes progress when he sticks his neck out.
JAMES BRYANT CONANT

Just for Fun

Judy and Gary had a Christmas tree farm. The first year they sold a number of trees. They received the same number of dollars for each tree as the number of trees they sold. When the season was over, they decided to divide the money. All of the money was in 10-dollar bills except for a few 1-dollar bills that did not total $10.00. Judy divided the bills by dealing them out alternately to herself and to Gary. Gary complained that Judy was unfair because she got both the first and the last bill. Gary said that Judy got $10.00 more than he did. Judy said that to make matters fair, she would let Gary have all of the 1-dollar bills. Gary argued that he was still being shortchanged. How much would Judy have to pay Gary to make things equal?

Our solution is in Appendix B.

8

Stratification

*Partitioning or Dividing Data
into Subsets*

Introduction

Stratification is a fancy word for looking at layers. For instance, a road is built of different layers. Envision the different-colored rocks, sand, gravel, and dirt that are revealed by a highway construction project. Each material has different characteristics. The principle of breaking things into component parts or layers can be applied to decision making. If we understand why things are as they are, then we have a basis for theorizing ways to make them better.

This chapter presents seven steps in stratification. Again, we draw an example from pie production. You can study pies by examining apple pies, custard pies, peach pies, and so forth independently to gain a better understanding of pies in general. What works with pies can help you with studying, checking into a hotel, manufacturing a car, teaching a class, collecting income tax, or whatever you do. All of these processes—and whatever you do—have inputs and outputs. They all can be broken down into strata or layers.

The good news is that you do not have to look at every input or every output. When you get a health checkup, the doctor does not remove all your blood;

she only takes a small sample. Sampling is looking at some of something, not all of it. A lot of information comes from samples. When you cook soup, you do not swallow the whole pot to see if it needs more salt; you take a taste test. The way you take the sample affects the quality of the information you receive about the whole. To get a random sample of the entire pot, you stir the soup before tasting it. The chapter ends with a simple and clear explanation of different ways to conduct sampling. As usual, we urge you to be creative in thinking about strata and sampling and adapting the concepts to help you in your process.

Why Things Are as They Are

Stratification separates data into subsets. There are many different possibilities for stratification groupings.

Stratification means putting like things together or separating data into subsets.

For example, even though we make fruit pies, they are not all alike. Cherry, apple, and blueberry pies are different. First, we identify similar types (such as vendor A, B, and C), methods (such as purchase, make, and subcontract), or groups (such as friends, family, and co-workers). Collecting data from each group or stratum allows us to compare them.

The purpose of stratifying data is to determine how each group affects the entire set of data. For instance, recall the example in Chapter 3 in which we looked at soldiers' heights. If we mixed men and women together in that example, we would not be able to estimate any soldier's height accurately. Here are some tips for stratifying data.

- ▶ Apply stratification only to variable data.
- ▶ Take at least 10 samples from each subgroup.
- ▶ Apply stratification only to distribution patterns that are not normal.
- ▶ Stratification is a technique for isolating and identifying the causes of problems.
- ▶ Stratification is a technique for improving processes that are currently working.
- ▶ Stratification can help you understand outcomes.

Steps in Stratification

Following are the seven steps in the stratification process.

Step 1. Determine what problem is negatively affecting your process. After selecting a problem, you must determine which variable is most likely responsible for it. You might use a designed experiment to do this or you might use some other tool such as brainstorming or a cause-and-effect diagram. Select a particular variable part of the process to investigate.

Step 2. Gather data about the variable part of the process. Collect the necessary variable data. You will need to decide how to collect and record the data. You may want to use a check sheet, as discussed in Chapter 1. For instance, you might want to collect attribute data about the pies' texture or variable data about the pies' weight.

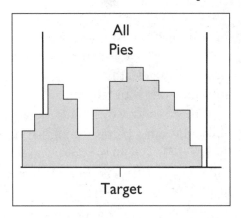

Step 3. Prepare a histogram from the data. At this point, prepare a histogram and determine if an abnormal frequency distribution is occurring. If the histogram shows an abnormal curve, proceed with stratification. If your histogram shows a normal curve, stratification will not help.

Step 4. Analyze the abnormal histogram. Try to determine the most likely cause of the abnormality and select a factor of production to stratify first. For example, you may decide that the moisture content of your fruit pies is varying from day to day. In that case, you would isolate this factor into the appropriate subpopulation grouping and proceed to stratify by this subpopulation.

Step 5. Arrange the data for the selected subpopulation. Once you have selected the factor you plan to isolate, you need to assemble the relative data for the appropriate group.

Step 6. Plot the histogram for each subpopulation selected. Now plot a histogram for each subpopulation you have chosen to investigate. In this case, plot a histogram for each of your three types of fruit pies.

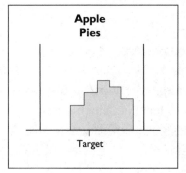

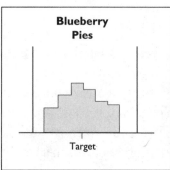

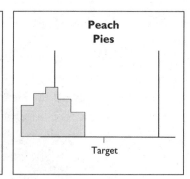

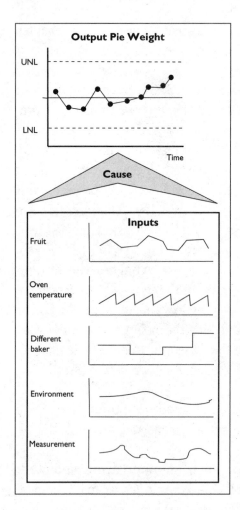

Step 7. Compare the histogram for each subpopulation with that for the total population. Now compare each subpopulation histogram with the total population histogram you prepared in Step 3. In this case, the peach pies are not within specifications. If all of the subpopulation histograms had displayed the normal curve and been within specifications, you would have had to identify a different potential cause and start over with Step 1.

Processes vary over time. A stable process exhibits the same pattern from one time period to the next. This stability allows you to predict what will happen. However, the fact that you can predict the kinds of pies that you will make does not mean that the pies you produce will be the kinds of pies you want.

Once your process is stable and repeatable, your challenge is to understand why things are as they are. Variation in result is caused by variation in input. This variation is seen in the upper and lower limits of the process. The limits exist because the incoming raw materials that you use to make your pies are not uniform. Fruit may come into your bakery with varying degrees of water content. Your tools and equipment will wear as time goes by. Your oven may not produce consistent heat, or it may burn out and require replacement. You have many bakers, and each one may have his or her own favorite way of making pies. The ambient temperature and humidity in your bakery will likely change with the seasons, days of the week, and hours of the day. Your measurement system itself may exhibit variation. You may not have a hard and fast way to measure the moisture of your pies. Each of these subprocesses may be a candidate for stratification.

Sampling

Recall that in Chapter 3 we measured one hundred Widgets. But that is doing it the hard way. You do not have to wait for a slack season to measure all of the Widgets you make. We just did that to demonstrate that the variation in any measurement will usually follow the bell-shaped normal pattern. An easier way to tell what is happening with your process is to take a sample.

A **sample** is a small number or quantity of what you produce. It represents your entire output.

Pick out a sample of five Widgets from that box of five hundred. No, no! Not all from the top layer! You need a random sample. Dig around in the box. Don't be accused of stacking the numbers.

Now measure these five Widgets. To ensure that you get a reasonable representation, get four more samples of five Widgets each. Be sure to take the samples in the same way. However, do not take all five samples at once. Spread the sample-taking time evenly across the entire eight-hour shift. Now, let's see what you got. The sample data is recorded on a file chart.

The averages of the five samples vary quite a bit from the target of 2.00 inches. We got the average for each sample by totaling the measurements for the entire sample and dividing by five. Then we added all five averages together and divided by the number of samples (5) to get the grand average— 2.001 inches. The grand average is also called the mean. We found the range for each sample by subtracting the smallest measurement in the sample from the largest measurement in the sample.

You will not always come quite so close to the actual average in five samples. However, if you have enough samples, the average of the samples will provide a very good estimate of the actual average of the lot. We recorded the samples on the file chart for transfer to a control chart. You could also record the readings directly on a control chart and save a step.

Sample Data					
Sample #1	Sample #2	Sample #3	Sample #4	Sample #5	
2.016	2.025	2.002*	1.973	2.033	
2.027*	1.963¤	1.988	2.046*	2.003	
1.994	2.015	1.999	1.941¤	2.037*	
1.954¤	2.059*	1.996	2.001	1.968¤	
1.985	1.990	1.987¤	2.009	2.013	Grand average
Average 1.995	2.010	1.993	1.994	2.011	2.001
Range .073	.096	.024	.105	.069	.073

* Largest measurement in sample
¤ Smallest measurement in sample

Random Sampling

Random "Of or designating a sample drawn from a population so that each member of the population has an equal chance to be drawn."

WEBSTER'S II NEW RIVERSIDE UNIVERSITY DICTIONARY

When you use stratification or conduct experiments, you generate a lot of data. A technique called random sampling lets you reduce your data to a manageable level while retaining all of the characteristics that your experiment originally generated.

When you collect data, remember:

▶ A sample is representative of an entire population only when it is random.

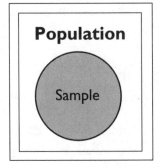

▶ Choosing a random sample allows you to make generalizations about the entire population based on information gathered from the sample.

▶ Understand your purpose for collecting data. This can help you determine which sampling technique is appropriate.

There are four different ways to collect data randomly. Some of them use a random number table, which is a table of numbers that a computer generates with no particular pattern. The purpose of using a random number table is to ensure that no bias enters into your sample selection. Some pocket calculators and most computers have random number generator keys built in.

Following are the sampling methods. Use the one that best meets your needs.

Simple Random Sampling

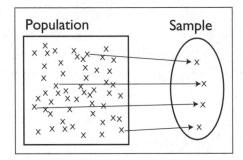

A simple random sample is produced when you choose the sample items one at a time from the entire population so that each member of the population has the same chance of being selected. Use simple random sampling anytime the items in a population can be listed without a great deal of effort. Simple random sampling involves using a random number table. Here are the steps to follow when using this method.

▶ Number the population.

▶ Decide on the sample size.

▶ Begin at a predetermined point on the table, starting at a different point on the table each time it is used. Move systematically through the table.

▶ Draw a sample of the desired size.

▶ Choose another number if the number chosen is a duplicate or if the number chosen falls outside of the population size.

Systematic Random Sampling

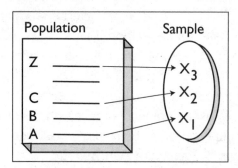

A systematic random sample is one in which every "nth" (for example, every 5th, 12th, 100th) item in the population is chosen for the sample. The population items must form some sort of sequence. Use this technique when it is not possible or convenient to list the entire population. Do not use it where the defects might form a pattern. Here are the steps to follow when using systematic random sampling.

▶ Decide on the sample size.
▶ Decide on the interval.
▶ Draw a sample of the desired size by selecting items in the chosen pattern.

For example, contact every 10th name in the phone book for a marketing survey to determine the kinds of pies consumers want to eat and what they would be willing to pay for them.

Stratified Random Sampling

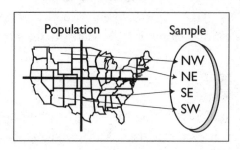

A stratified random sample is produced from subgroups or strata in the population designated on a basis relevant to the sampling study. Elements within each stratum should be similar. The differences between strata should be great.

Use stratified random sampling when logically dividing a population into subgroups. This will make the process less time-consuming. Here are the steps to follow when using this method.

▶ Decide on logical subgroups.
▶ Decide on the sample size within each subgroup.
▶ Draw a sample of the desired size from each subgroup, using a random number table.

Cluster Random Sampling

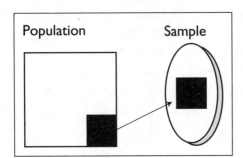

A cluster random sample results when you randomly choose several subgroups within the population and include all or some members of each subgroup in the sample. Use cluster random sampling when it is more convenient to select items as a group rather than individually. Here are steps to follow when using stratified random sampling.

▶ Decide how the population could be grouped for ease of sampling.
▶ Decide on the sample size.
▶ Select at random entire subgroups, using a random number table.
▶ Analyze all items in, or a random sample of items from, each group selected.

For example, interview all of the people on just one street in a housing development to study the entire development.

A Different Type of Partitioning

Partitioning can help you decide how to spend your time, money, and resources. Vilfredo Pareto, an Italian economist (1848–1923), studied the distribution of wealth of the world and found a significant pattern. A few people had most of the money. For example, in the United States in 1996, 17 percent of the people controlled 77 percent of the publicly held stocks. This way of looking at the distribution of wealth leads to a special pattern called the Pareto principle.

The **Pareto principle** says that about 80 percent of the results come from about 20 percent of the causes.

Roughly 80 percent of the goals scored in the National Hockey League are scored by 20 percent of the players. Apply this principle in your world, and you'll find that 20 percent of your customers are generating 80 percent of the complaints. If you identify these vital few, then you can find ways to make your customers happy. Application of the Pareto principle is a major tool for determining when and where to make improvements.

Pareto diagrams are used to analyze data from a new perspective, to focus attention on problems in priority order, to compare data changes during different time periods, and to provide a basis for showing the cumulative effect of a problem. A Pareto diagram provides an easy-to-see graphical comparison. Geometric shapes are easier to compare than verbal descriptions. A Pareto chart gives you a starting point for examining a situation.

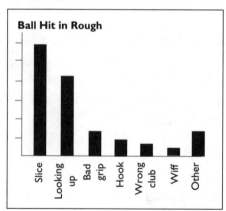

The sample Pareto chart shows information about a golfer's problems. You can easily see that the first two issues (20%) cause almost 80 percent of the golfer's scoring problems. If he can solve his slice and keep from looking up, he will have made a significant improvement in his golf game and reduced his score significantly.

Partitioning or stratifying can save you a great deal of time and effort. Be careful to make your samples random, or you will fail to see patterns that you should see, and you will see patterns that really do not exist. Using a simple tool such as the Pareto chart can help you focus your resources on the areas where they will be most beneficial.

Stratification is the process of arranging things that are similar. You identify similar things by type. Collecting data for each group or stratum allows you to compare. If a distribution is not normal, stratification may be misleading!

Using proper sampling techniques can increase your success in making decisions with the aid of numbers. Remember:

► A sample is representative of an entire population only when it is random.

► Choosing a random sample allows you to make generalizations about the entire population based on information gathered from the sample.

► Use a Pareto chart to stratify your data.

► If you do not understand your purpose in collecting data, you may collect the wrong data.

► Determine which sampling technique is appropriate.

There are two different kinds of errors. One error is failing to make a change when something should be changed; the other is changing something that does not need to be changed.

Just for Fun

Dan and Carolyn played games all evening. They were playing for $10.00 per game. At the end of the evening, Dan had lost $30.00. He had won three games. How many games did the couple play? How many games did Carolyn win?

The answer is in Appendix B.

9

Relationships

Identifying Cause and Effect

Introduction

What causes what? Does rain cause corn to grow, or does corn growing cause rain to fall? Obviously, rain causes corn to grow. If you get more rain, you get more corn, up to a point. Then, at some point, you have a lake, not a cornfield. The cause-and-effect relationship between two variables can yield powerful insights that help you identify and understand why things behave as they do.

Note: As with measurement, the power is not in the numbers. It is in the use to which the numbers are put. Understanding comes from the person using the numbers, not the numbers themselves. The goal is not more data, more numbers, or more measurement; rather, it is better understanding, better decisions, and better results.

The results you get are traceable to specific causes. Identify those causes. Collect measurements of the relationship between the results and the causes. Draw a picture of the relationship with a scatter diagram. This chapter outlines a step-by-step method for drawing a scatter diagram. (A computer can draw one in a fraction of a second.) Sometimes you may have to look at several scatter diagrams until you find one that reveals why things are as they are. The second part of the chapter provides guidelines for interpreting scatter diagrams and explains the importance of correlation.

Uncovering Meaningful Relationships

Everyone experiences relationships on a daily basis.

This is a sample of the text for the definition, or these are more synonyms and usages that are commonly found in the English language.

The **scatter diagram** is a tool for studying the possible relationship between two different things that can change.

These things that change are made up of sets of numbers, which are called variables because they can change or vary. For instance, we could measure the frequency with which we see beards on men and the rise and fall of the stock market. The scatter diagram is a graphic display of many points that represent the relationship between two different variables. It gives you insight into a possible cause-and-effect relationship. It cannot prove that one variable causes the other, but it does make it clear whether a relationship exists and how strong the relationship is.

For example, when you bake a pie, changing the oven temperature affects the baking time. Knowledge of a relationship can often provide a clue to the solution of a problem. By using a scatter diagram, you can determine if a relationship appears to exist between two variables. This knowledge leads to a method of controlling output.

A scatter diagram allows you to investigate two variables that you think might be related. For example, you may want to investigate the relationship between the fruit and the moisture content of your pies. Such relationships play an important part in any process. By understanding the nature of these relationships, you can make your process more efficient.

How to Construct a Scatter Diagram

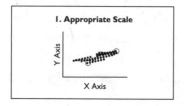

1. Select two variables that you think are related. Gather the necessary data for both variables. It is important to collect enough data. Usually you should have at least 30 numbers.

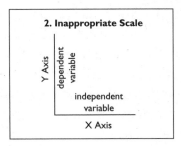

2. Inappropriate Scale

2. Prepare graph paper. First, find the range for each of the variables. After you know the ranges, select the appropriate scale for your graph. The scale must include all the numbers you need to plot. Choose your independent and dependent variables to plot.

An **independent variable** is a value that affects the dependent variable.

A **dependent variable** is a value that is determined by the independent variable.

For example, rain causes crops to grow, but the growing crops do not cause rain. Rain is the independent variable, and the crop yield is the dependent variable. It is not always possible to determine what the dependent and independent variables are before you have collected the data. In such a case, make your most informed guess, and put what you believe will be the independent variable on the X axis.

An expanded Y axis, as shown in the illustration, definitely improves the usefulness of the scatter diagram. Because the values for the Y scale are concentrated in a small area, the scale has been expanded to accommodate only those values. Now the relationship between the X and Y variables is easier to see.

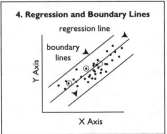

3. Expanded Y Axis

3. Plot your data onto the diagram. If two points happen to fall at the same place, draw a circle around the original point to indicate that another point has landed at the same position.

4. Draw a pair of boundary lines along the outer edge of the data points. Add a line in the middle of the boundary lines. This is called the regression line.

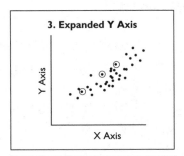

4. Regression and Boundary Lines

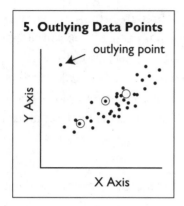

5. Another consideration in constructing a scatter diagram is to watch for points on the diagram that do not seem to belong to the rest of the data. They appear to be outside the general pattern of the other data points. Chances are that something was different about that item or that an error was made in its measurement. Be careful not to be misled by these outlying data points. On the other hand, do not ignore them if they are valid.

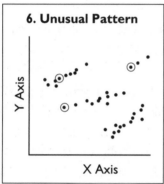

6. If you encounter an unusual pattern like that in the illustration, do not immediately conclude that there is no relationship between the variables. Double-check the data to make sure that it does not represent more than one population. You need to draw a separate diagram for each population.

Interpret your scatter diagram. Look for patterns, using the guidelines that follow.

How to Interpret Scatter Diagrams

There are five patterns that you will usually encounter in scatter diagrams. They are not the only possible patterns, but most scatter diagrams will resemble one of them.

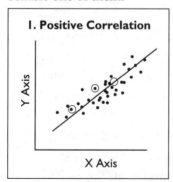

1. The first relationship pattern is a positive correlation, where both numbers increase at the same time. When X goes up, so does Y. Therefore, if X is controlled, Y should be controlled also. A perfect positive correlation is found in the length of a carpet plotted in inches against the length of carpet in feet. When the length in inches increases, so does the length in feet.

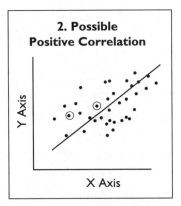

2. The second pattern shows a possible positive relationship. If the value of X increases, the value of Y tends to increase also. The diagram does not show a strong, clear pattern for the positive linear relationship. This means that if the value of X is increased, the value of Y increases somewhat, but the value of Y also seems to be influenced by other causes. An example of possible positive correlation is the relationship between people's heights and their weights. The taller people are, the more they tend to weigh; shorter people tend to weigh less. These are average findings—thus the name *scatter* diagram. If you plot the heights and weights of 20 of your friends, you will see that the weights vary. The miles your colleagues drive to work and their commuting times will be positively correlated in this same way, as will the age of a car and the number of miles on its odometer.

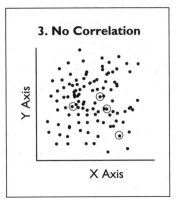

3. The third pattern shows no discernible relationship between the variables. It looks like the pattern from a shotgun shell. This pattern often reflects the assumptions of many direct-mail marketers. They send out lots of advertising, hoping that some of it will be effective. An example of absence of correlation is the value of the Dow Jones Index plotted on a daily basis versus the number of runs scored by the New York Yankees every day during the baseball season.

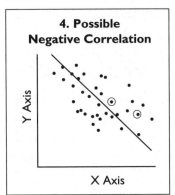

4. In the fourth pattern, there is evidence of a possible negative linear relationship. The Y value seems to decrease as the value of X increases. Although the relationship between the two variables is somewhat vague, there is still enough of a pattern to suggest a negative relationship. You might find a negative corre-

lation like this between your golf scores and the number of hours you practice. The more you practice, the lower your golf scores should be.

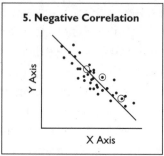

5. Negative Correlation

Y Axis

X Axis

5. The fifth common pattern shows a definite negative linear relationship. As the value of X increases, the value of Y decreases. An example of negative correlation is the fact that the faster you drive over 70 miles per hour, the fewer miles per gallon your car gets. Therefore, the faster you drive, the less efficient your car is in terms of gas mileage.

Generally, scatter diagrams are used to investigate such relationships as weight versus strength, temperature versus moisture content, and so forth. However, you can use scatter diagrams to search for types of relationships such as an individual's effectiveness in relation to the training they receive.

Use a scatter diagram if you suspect that there is a relationship between two different variables. The scatter diagram can help you to
▶ Determine if there is a relationship between two variables and
▶ Quantify the relationship between two variables.
When you use a scatter diagram, remember:
▶ Be careful not to incorporate more than one population into your data set.
▶ The more data you plot, the clearer the relationship will be.
▶ Don't ignore data that does not fit with your theory.
▶ Be sure to examine different potential relationships.
If you look at the wrong relationships, you can wind up with the wrong answer. You can easily misuse this tool to prove your favorite theory.

Just for Fun

Ruth was going on a trip to visit her grandchildren. She decided to take $1,000 with her. She asked the cashier at the bank to put the money into 10 different colored envelopes so that each sealed envelope would contain a different amount of money. If Ruth used different combinations of her colored envelopes, she could create any sum from $1 to $1,000. How did the cashier divide the money among the envelopes?

If you would like to check your answer, one solution is in Appendix B.

10

Implementation

Applying What You Have Learned

Introduction

Building a bridge between theory and practice is easier said than done. This chapter is our bridge from theory to practice. Having spent the 1980s and '90s helping organizations implement statistical thinking, we have developed a model. Like all models it is imperfect, but we hope you will find it useful. Use our model to create a model for ways to use statistical thinking in your organization.

All organizations are different. Yet all organizations—whether public or private, large or small, manufacturing or service—have one thing in common. They are collections of people. People use measurement. The people path, then, is the only way to achieve better results and make better decisions. The path to improvement leads to statistical process improvement, or SPI for short. SPI is a combination of measurement and people working to make things better. This chapter outlines a set of team structures and activities that can be used to drive the SPI effort in your organization. Finally, however, it is your organization, and what happens is up to you. We cannot tell you what to do. We cannot even tell you what to think. But we can help you identify some things to think about when using numbers to make better decisions.

Putting It All Together

The leading cause of customer discontent is variation, which means getting something that you did not want. A fancy way to describe it is as an unforeseen deviation from an anticipated or expected set of results. Variation in your product's quality often results in waste, which in turn results in your becoming less efficient. You are less efficient because of lost time and material.

An input that varies causes your output to vary. As a result, your customers look elsewhere, and your reputation suffers. Everything you give to someone else is your output; what you get from someone else is your input. For instance, when you take someone to a movie theater, the guest is your customer, and your output is a trip to the movies. You may receive your input by looking in the newspaper or telephoning the theater to find out what time the movie is playing. If you get the wrong information about the starting time, you may miss the feature. You receive bad input and the consequence is bad output, resulting in an unhappy customer (your guest). Your customer may choose to look elsewhere next time because of an input that varied.

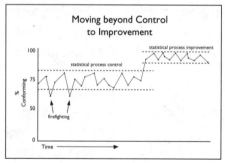

You can bring about more rapid improvement in whatever you do if you use numbers to make decisions. Organizations that use team-oriented problem solving believe in getting everyone involved. Organizations often have entire programs focused on statistical process control. Instead, we recommend following the statistical process improvement (SPI) path to move beyond mere control-based results to improved results.

The prime objective in following the statistical process improvement path is to become more effective by using numbers to make better decisions.

The effectiveness of processes is reduced by two types of variation: common cause variation and special cause variation.

Common cause variation results from a set of variables that have been designed into the system.

This type of variation stems from such causes as mandated speed, process design, multiple supplies, schedules, and training efficiency.

Special cause variation occurs when all planned factors are in place but something nevertheless goes wrong.

The use of statistical tools and thinking to reduce process variation has proven extremely effective. You can reduce common cause variation by decreasing the amount of variation designed into a process. You can avoid special cause variation by making everyone aware of special causes when they occur and the actions taken to correct them.

Drastic reduction of variation in product and processes provides many benefits, including the following:

▶ An increase in efficiency, which means more output for the same or less input.

▶ An improvement in what you send to your customers. This results in an increase in customer satisfaction. As a result, you become a more valuable supplier.

▶ A reduction in waste. This results in an improvement in both cost-effectiveness and timeliness in meeting schedules. It also provides cost savings.

▶ A long-term overall improvement in reputation.

The SPI path involves the use of simple tools. In this book, we have addressed the simple statistical tools that are most commonly used and that are directly related to monitoring of process output and performance. It is best to train everyone in the application of statistical techniques, conducting that training on a just-in-time basis. Learning and use are connected—people learn best by doing. Training should be relevant and timely. In fact, the best way to learn something is to teach it to someone else.

The SPI path is really a way of thinking, not just a set of tools. The statistical tools and methods presented in this book are only the tip of the iceberg. However, some tools get used significantly more often than others—as in woodworking, most people use a hammer more often than a drill press.

There are many other tools and techniques. Thanks to the ubiquity of computers, arithmetic is no longer a stumbling block to using numbers appropriately. In this book we have addressed the tools that use numbers. In addition, on the SPI path, you will often find that you need to address ideas, concepts, and beliefs. There are many other tools for addressing these issues. We will very briefly describe some of them. The bibliography lists some reference books that contain further relevant information. In addition, many of these word manipulation tools are featured in our book *Mind Expanders: Provoking Creativity in Individuals and Organizations*, another book in this series. The tools in that book, which focuses on creativity, can be used in multiple ways and can help you solve some of your problems creatively.

Following are the seven most frequently used tools:

1. **Pareto chart.** Lists events in order, from most occurrences to fewest. Use this bar chart to set priorities.
2. **Flow chart.** Creates a picture of a process from start to end; it shows all major elements of a process in sequence; highlights the major decision points. Decision points usually have the greatest impact on operating costs. These points provide opportunities for improvement.
3. **Histogram.** Graphically displays all the data so that a feel for the precision and accuracy of the data can be developed.
4. **Cause-and-effect diagram.** Organizes the thinking process and facilitates group dynamics during brainstorming sessions.
5. **Scatter diagram.** Plots points against each other to help you search for relationships.
6. **Run chart.** Tracks process performance over time.
7. **Control chart.** Helps you establish process capability, view the process for stability, and search for causes of variation.

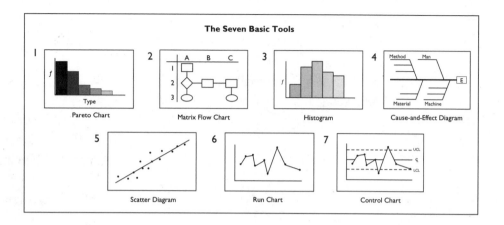

Today's fast-paced, highly competitive global marketplace requires that you be both efficient and effective. Being efficient means that you get more output and use less input. Being effective means that you give your customers what they want.

Statistics, or numbers, are something everyone uses in daily life, both on and off the job. When you talk about the weather or the Dow Jones Average, you are using statistics. What role do statistics play in the SPI program? Webster's International Dictionary of the English Language defines statistics as follows:

The science of the systematic collection, organization, and mathematical analysis of quantifiable data so as to present descriptive information about the data, to induce characteristics of a larger population of which the data is construed as representative, or to infer the significance of underlying factors whose effects are reflected in the data.

Although this imposing definition may help you understand the word *statistics,* it is somewhat misleading in our context. First, the SPI path is not just about statistics. It is about people. It is about people managing processes, creating products, and producing something for someone. It is about people working together to attain the mutual goals of a collectively successful organization. It is about people creating individually satisfying personal careers. Perhaps most important, it is about people working in an environment that encourages them to solve problems, using the experiences they have accumulated. We believe that statistics as used on the SPI path

▶ Are an objective language for communication,
▶ Provide a quantification of what is occurring, and
▶ Provide insights into patterns and relationships.

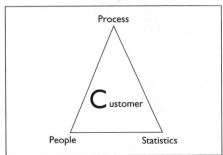

SPI tools provide a nonthreatening, communicative language that encourages problem solving and decision making. The SPI path must be developed along two parallel and equally exciting routes:

▶ A people route and
▶ A statistical route.

The People Route

The people route leads to an atmosphere of cooperation and team building throughout the organization. The statistical route uses the nonthreatening language of communication called statistics. Both routes, though requiring different skills, are merged to achieve synergy. The result of this merger is an environment in which individuals from diverse areas are drawn into the problem-solving and decision-making processes. Using the SPI path effectively requires an orientation different from that typical of most organizations in the past. The SPI path forces people to attempt change in

▶ Purpose (why we do what we do),
▶ Attitudes (how we feel about what we do), and
▶ Behaviors (what we are doing).

The purpose of an organization is set by its executives; it determines the visible vector of the organization. Your individual purpose determines the direction you follow. In addition, it is important—especially for individuals—to keep the larger purpose in mind.

Attitudes are nebulous. They are usually hard to define and usually resistant to change. The reason attitudes are so difficult to change directly is that an attitude is the product of thousands, maybe hundreds of thousands of

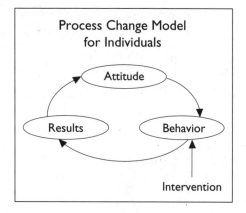

Process Change Model
for Individuals

observed results. Some of these results are small and some are large. They have occurred over the person's total experience, both on and off the job. Thus, attitudes are extremely complex. They are subject to change, but you cannot address them directly.

Behavior drives results. Unlike attitudes, behaviors can be changed directly and quickly, given the proper intervention. A rapid change in results will follow. As individuals begin to see changed results (reinforced by the perceived need for change), they will begin to change their attitudes as they reevaluate their attitudes on the basis of their new experiences. Only management can change the systems and processes in an organization.

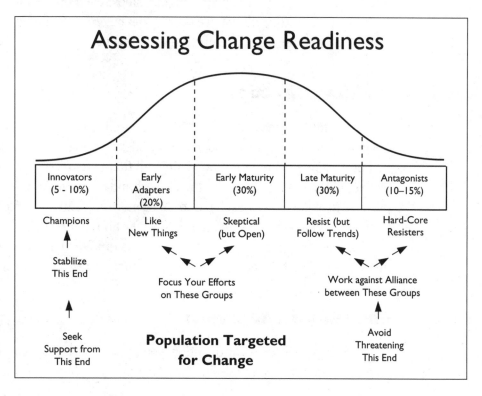

Assessing Change Readiness

Innovators (5 - 10%)	Early Adapters (20%)	Early Maturity (30%)	Late Maturity (30%)	Antagonists (10–15%)
Champions	Like New Things	Skeptical (but Open)	Resist (but Follow Trends)	Hard-Core Resisters

Stabliize This End

Focus Your Efforts on These Groups

Work against Alliance between These Groups

Seek Support from This End

Population Targeted for Change

Avoid Threatening This End

Use the breakthroughs and savings from the initial projects to validate the SPI process. A transformation to SPI does not occur spontaneously in every stratum of the organization. The SPI effort must start with the positive innovators focusing on the Early Adapters and Early Maturity groups. Systems must be in place to empower individuals as appropriate in the context of the SPI path.

Knowledge is not a necessary and sufficient condition for its application.
    Bob Reid

The Statistical Route

The statistical route provides a step-by-step way of using the many available SPI tools. The SPI path has seven basic steps, each one lending itself to a number of tools. You will not use every tool at every step. Some tools may be used more than once on the same issue. Following are the seven basic steps.

Defining Direction

It is important to know what you are supposed to do. Although this seems obvious, it is the most overlooked and underacknowledged concept of SPI. Just providing a good definition is often all that is required. For example, do we just bake pies, or are we in the dessert and snack food business? Is our purpose to make better peach pies or to be more efficient and effective in baking pies? Is our purpose to expand into a new and different product line? Are we looking to acquire a company or to be acquired? The answers to these questions will influence the types of result that we are looking for.

Choosing an Approach

Once you have defined your direction, you must choose the approach you are going to take. You need to decide how you will get where you want to go.

The most common approach is the analytical one. When you analyze something, you break it down into its component parts. Although this is the most frequently used approach, it often leads to maximizing efficiency of processes that should not exist. We usually are overwhelmed with details that limit our thinking and creativity. For instance, if we break an egg and analyze each of its component parts, we can develop a chicken feed that will make the shell harder and reduce breakage.

Another approach, systems thinking, helps us look at the context within which we work. This approach means looking at our situation in relation to the overall system of which it is a part. When we choose the systems approach, we are looking to maximize effectiveness. That is, we are deciding whether our process should exist before we make it more efficient. Using a systems approach for the egg problem produces a different result. As bakers, we are looking for eggs that are easy to use. Instead of a shell that is harder to break, we are looking for one that breaks easily but doesn't shatter. This requirement presents a much different problem for the egg producer.

Building a Model

Building a model is a way of understanding a system, a process, or one or more functions. The model becomes our control sample. There are many different types of models.

Most communications occur through models. Many models consist of words; however, the majority are visual. Remember the first model of the solar system you saw in school? What would the weather forecaster do without a weather map? The map is a model. We can construct a variety of models to show what something is or is not. The model may represent what we want something to be or what we would like to occur. For example, we might photograph the perfect pie, then compare each pie that we bake to this control sample.

All models are wrong; some models are useful.
George Box

Generating Ideas

When we generate ideas, we do so looking either backward or forward. We ask, "What went right or wrong?" or "What should we do?" There are many types of tools for idea generation; simple tools are the best. Many of them are described in our book on creativity, *Mind Expanders: Provoking Creativity in Individuals and Organizations.*

For our bakery, generating ideas might mean developing several new types of products such as meat pies, hand-held individual fruit pies, and fried bananas on a stick.

When you are generating ideas, you are not judging whether they are good or bad. You are just trying to brainstorm a large number of possibilities. What you are generating ideas about depends on your definition of direction, the approach you have chosen, and the model you have developed.

Prioritizing Possibilities

The need to prioritize possibilities arises many times every day. Examples on the SPI path include deciding what issue to pursue, narrowing the field of possible causes, and deciding which possible solution to implement.

When we prioritized the possibilities we generated in Step 4, we decided to develop a hand-held fruit pie. In addition, we decided to research the market for a banana on a stick. We do not contemplate going into the meat pie business because we believe that our niche is in the fruit product business.

Measuring Performance

Measurements track process performance over time. They enable you to tell if something is wrong or if what you have done has improved the process. Measurements provide a clear idea of how well a process is working. Each measure should be focused on what your customer is looking for, not what you can do. We have devoted a considerable portion of this book to introducing some tools for assessing how well your process is doing. You should develop performance measures when your process is begun. You may need to change or eliminate them over time as you learn what they are really telling you.

We have several performance measures in our pie business. The first thing we measure is how the pie turns out: The consistency must be just right. This measure is important to the customer who buys the pie. The second thing we measure is how many pies we produce for each pound of fruit that we buy. This measure is important to our shareholder customer. The third thing we measure is how satisfied our employees are. This is important to our employee customers. We have many other measures, each one focusing on a specific customer's need.

Developing a Plan

Planning results in a consistent approach to achieving your objective. Without a well-thought-out plan, any change you make will initially appear to yield positive results. However, without a plan, you cannot take account of everything involved in the change.

For example, if you decide to produce a hand-held individual fruit pie, where do you begin? Do you first develop a recipe, or do you begin by marketing the product? Do you buy different fruit or use what you have? Do you need new packaging equipment, or can you use your current packaging? Although these are obvious issues, developing a well-thought-out, detailed plan will help you find and understand all of the smaller connected issues before you encounter them. A plan will save you considerable time and resources.

Keeping on Track

Statistical tools help you decide what to do. If what is done does not coincide with what you want, it is up to you to formulate a new approach to bring reality into line with your visible vector. Your visible vector includes your values, beliefs, and mores and your vision for where you are moving.

It has been estimated that as many as 95 percent of all problems within an organization can be solved through the people route and the statistical route.

Information based on facts is useful because it can show you when

▶ Reality and visible vector coincide. This is what you want.

▶ Reality and visible vector don't coincide. You can now take steps to make them coincide.

Your **visible vector** is a combination that includes where you want to go with your values, mores, and competencies.

The SPI path can help whether or not the reality coincides with your visible vector. If you know where you are going and are working hard to get there, the SPI path will help keep you on track. If you are not on track, the SPI path can help you get back on track. However, it is very hard to hit a target if you don't know what it is. If you have no idea what you want to do, the SPI path will be of little help to you.

An important feature of SPI path information is that the results are impersonal. Most people believe that these concepts are a way of pointing the finger at someone, of attributing responsibility for a problem to someone else. This is not the case at all! People who follow the SPI path learn to maximize their own efficiency and effectiveness. They learn to resolve problems by looking at the process, not at the individuals involved in the process. In addition, by keeping the focus impersonal, participants can concentrate on pinpointing and implementing constructive changes rather than worrying about past failures or feeling threatened by external criticism. This is why the SPI path provides a nonthreatening language for communication.

Using Statistics in Organizations

The goal of using statistics is to get where you want to go by reducing variation and driving processes to meet their targets. How do you do this? Many organizations' structures reflect a do-what-you're-told approach to getting things done. When this is the case, it is virtually impossible to implement a program like SPI. In that type of organization, there is no opportunity or motivation for individuals to become involved in the problem-solving process. On the other hand, many organizations are struggling with the question of how to encourage individuals to use their hidden abilities and creativity to

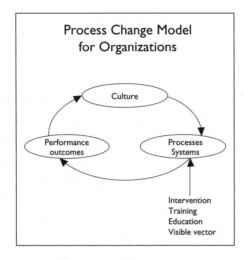

Process Change Model for Organizations

make appropriate decisions and solve problems. Another key question is how much individual empowerment is appropriate. These issues are often not faced during downsizing, rightsizing, and reengineering. It is possible to deal with all of these issues on the SPI path.

When an organization decides to implement SPI fully, many changes in responsibility will occur. A typical timeline for implementing a SPI program is shown in the matrix below.

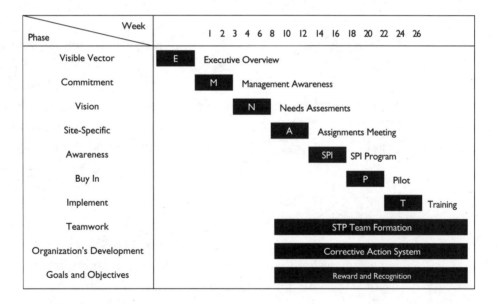

Training makes the changes easier to implement. Implementing the SPI process in an organization involves seven stages of training in which individuals or groups work under the direction of an SPI steering committee made up of high-level managers. Team coordinators enhance interaction between groups. A high degree of interaction between groups will help forestall surprises and problems down the road. Following are descriptions of the seven stages of training. In the illustration corresponding to each stage, the individuals affected at that stage are represented by symbols set in black boxes.

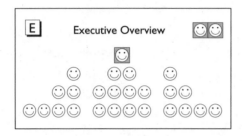

Executive overview. Senior management gives their view of a visible vector to be developed for the organization. A visible vector includes but is not limited to the values, beliefs, and mores of the organization and the direction in which it is moving.

Management awareness seminar. The SPI tools and philosophy are introduced to individuals who will actually work on implementation or whose direct or indirect support is required. This seminar provides the initial exposure to SPI, although some prerequisite reading by the participants is required.

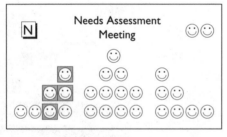

Needs assessment meeting. The needs assessment meeting takes place shortly after the management awareness seminar. Its purpose is to ensure that the organization is committed to the SPI training process. Specific goals for the meeting are to design the training manual for the organization and to develop a list of actions for implementation according to the time line.

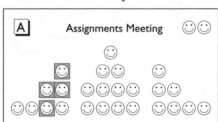

Assignments meeting. The assignments meeting takes place one month after the needs assessment meeting. Its purpose is to develop organization-specific examples for the SPI training manual. In addition, the leader may discuss the philosophy and practice of SPI implementation and the time line, and promote actual use of the SPI tools. Everyone should be encouraged to become familiar with them.

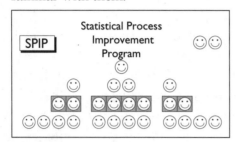

Statistical process improvement program. This is a one-day multimedia presentation to train supervisors to conduct a $1\frac{1}{2}$ hour presentation for all associates. It is an awareness session that precedes actual associate training. The first $1\frac{1}{2}$ hours consist of the presentation itself. In the last $4\frac{1}{2}$ hours, supervisors are trained to present the material.

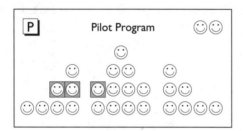

Pilot program. In the pilot program, participants are trained in SPI philosophy, concepts, and tools. This is the first real test of the tools and examples developed during previous sessions.

Associate training sessions. The associate training sessions cover all aspects of SPI philosophy, tools, and techniques, from the conceptual aspects to the practical, job-specific aspects.

Each stage of training entails a particular level of involvement on the part of the participants. Each stage presents a particular aspect of the overall process in logical order. Each stage requires its own training sessions.

Organizing for SPI

Organizations that successfully implement the SPI process involve their key personnel in distinct ways. Each part of the organization has specific duties and responsibilities. Successful organizations use different types of teams. The primary responsibilities of each team are as follows:

SPI Leadership Team (LT). The LT is responsible for overall implementation of the SPI process. They are also responsible for making sure that the program is working as designed.

Task Team (TT). The primary responsibility of the TT is to ensure the smooth and unhindered training of participants in the SPI process. They are also in charge of all preparations required for the training sessions. In addition, they are responsible for analyzing the process after implementation.

Short-Term Project Team (STP). The STP consists of four to nine subject matter experts who work on a problem until it is solved. When the problem is solved, the team is dissolved. No STP should exist for longer than four months.

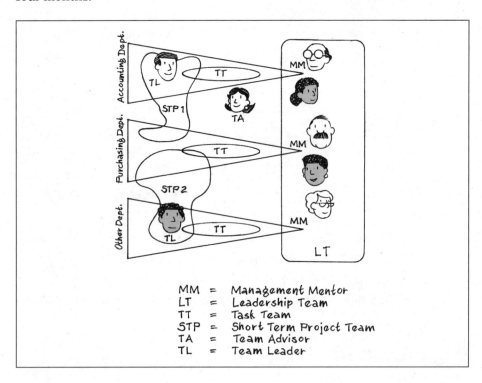

MM	=	Management Mentor
LT	=	Leadership Team
TT	=	Task Team
STP	=	Short Term Project Team
TA	=	Team Advisor
TL	=	Team Leader

Because the responsibilities of the LT are so vital, we will describe them in more detail. The LT is responsible for overall implementation of the SPI process in an organization. The team consists of the highest-ranking manager and selected members of his or her staff. Those selected for participation should have some direct involvement to facilitate maximum communication between related areas.

The responsibilities for the LT include the following:

▶ Creating a time line for the conversion to SPI,
▶ Specifying the initial applications,
▶ Appointing and supporting SPI team coordinator(s),
▶ Appointing and training the project team leader(s),
▶ Appointing TT members, and
▶ Ensuring that appointments to the TT are maintained.

The LT must develop a charter and a time line for overall implementation of SPI. The time line should take into account the number of participants, their schedules, and the projected requirements for the coming year. The time line may be extended to two years if appropriate. The chart gives an overview of the relationships between teams.

Team Relationships

	LT	TT	STP
• Name	Leadership Team (LT)	Task Team (TT)	Short-Term Project Team (STP)
• Function	Oversee implementation of SPI	Monitor a process	Solve a problem
• Leader	Plant manager	Elected	Selected
• Membership	MT	Subset of impacted area	Potential (anyone related to the problem)
• Duration	Ongoing	Ongoing	3–4 months
• Frequency of meeting	Once a month	Every two weeks	As needed (intensive)

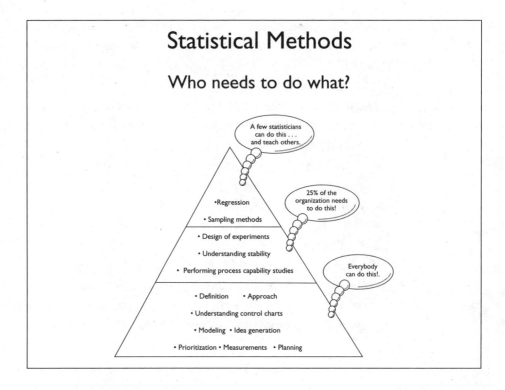

At the end of the training sessions, all participants should know how to apply specific SPI tools in their areas as soon as they return to their regular jobs. If possible, each one should have a copy of this book. It will help to reinforce the participants' newly acquired knowledge and help them immediately begin applying the knowledge to their jobs. The tools described in this book are appropriate for any given process. You can use them by themselves, as part of an SPC program, or as you proceed down the SPI path. Good luck!

Individuals use numbers in decision making and problem solving differently than organizations do. This chapter looks both at how individuals make decisions and how an organization can make numbers part of the way it does business.

Variation results either from a common cause or from a special cause. In either case, something goes wrong. Both types of variation occur for individuals and organizations alike. Drastic reduction of variation in product and processes provides many benefits, including

▶ An increase in efficiency,

▶ An improvement in what you provide your customers,

▶ A reduction in waste, and

▶ A long-term overall improvement in reputation.

The SPI Path must be developed along two parallel and equally exciting routes:

▶ A people route and

▶ A statistical route.

The SPI Path can work for your organization if you understand that

▶ It is not possible to mandate change; change requires leadership, and that

▶ Statistics cannot solve a problem—only people can. Statistics can only help you decide what you should pursue.

Tools should be used only when they provide benefit. They should not be force-fit to every situation. It is up to you to decide when to use numbers to make decisions. Numbers provide data, which is the basis of most decisions. Use it wisely!

Just for Fun

Nancy invites Paul, Joan, and Jenette over to her house for an afternoon of games. When everyone arrives, they decide to find out who plays what games. Nancy plays all of the games she names; however, Paul does not play basketball. Two of Nancy's friends play basketball. Two play baseball, and two play badminton. Jenette plays badminton. The one who does not play badminton does not play basketball. The one who does not play baseball does not play basketball. Which games does Paul play? Which games does Joan play? Which games does Jenette play? Which games does Nancy play?

If you would like to check your answer, one solution is in Appendix B.

More About Control Charts

Why Control Charts Look the Way They Do

In Chapter 5, we promised you details on constructing a control chart. That is the purpose of this appendix. We will visit a widget factory and take you step by step through control chart construction.

	Sample #1	Sample #2	Sample #3	Sample #4	Sample #5	
	2.016	2.025	2.002*	1.973	2.033	
	2.027*	1.963¤	1.988	2.046*	2.003	
	1.994	2.015	1.999	1.941¤	2.037*	
	1.954¤	2.059*	1.996	2.001	1.968¤	
	1.985	1.990	1.987¤	2.009	2.013	Grand
						Average
Average	1.995	2.010	1.993	1.994	2.011	2.001
Range	.073	.096	.024	.105	.069	.073

* Largest measurement in sample
¤ Smallest measurement in sample

This range is the difference between the largest and smallest measurement in the sample. Statisticians use the letter R to represent range, so we will use that symbol. The range varies from sample to sample. The average of the ranges is 0.0734.

In a lot of 100 Widgets, we could divide the range by six to get the standard deviation, but we cannot do this calculation with samples of only five. In the big lot, there are 100 chances of getting some of the extreme values. In a sample of only five, there is much less chance of getting these extreme values. In a small sample, we must divide by a smaller number.

We call this number d_2. You can find the appropriate factor for any sample size in the table on page 151. In the same table, you will also find several other factors. We will explain them when we get to the step-by-step directions for making a control chart. These factors have been developed over many years. Don't worry about what they mean. Everyone who uses them just looks them up in a table.

For samples of five, the d_2 factor is 2.33. Dividing the average range, 0.0734, by 2.33 gives us a standard deviation of 0.0315. That does not differ much from the figure of 0.030 that you get by using all 100 pieces to compute the standard deviation. Remember that statisticians use shorthand to describe things. They place a — on top of a number for average. So instead of using the term *average range,* they would simply use the figure $\overline{R}$.

Our example is a good demonstration of the fact that, by taking relatively few samples, you can find out two very important things about the distribution of the measurements of any product: the average ($\overline{x}$), and the standard deviation (σ).

The σ (sigma) of your Widgets is 0.03 inches, and the $\overline{x}$ (average) is 2.00 inches. Knowing these two values, you can now put some percentage figures on your old friend the distribution curve. Your Widget distribution produces a normal curve.

If you are doing a good job of cutting your Widgets to the specification of 2.00 inches, 68 percent should be between 2.00 inches minus one σ, and 2.00 inches plus one σ, or between 1.97 inches and 2.03 inches.

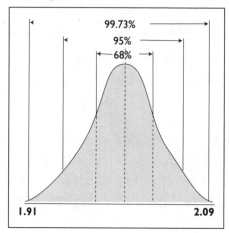

95 percent of your Widgets should be between minus 2σ and plus 2σ, or between 1.94 inches and 2.06 inches. Then 99.73 percent should be between minus 3σ and plus 3σ, or between 1.91 inches and 2.09 inches.

Even if something very unusual should happen to give you an occasional Widget shorter than 1.91 inches or longer than 2.09 inches, your process is still in control. As long as all of your Widget-cutting machines are properly adjusted to produce the average of 2.00 inches, you could give odds of 997 to 3 that anyone could not walk into the factory and pick up one at random that would fall outside the limits.

Unfortunately, however, machines, materials, and operators do not always do what they are supposed to do. Take Scott Jones on number 2 machine as an example. Scott's mother-in-law has been camping at his house for the last six weeks, and Scott has been feeling rather frustrated. His mind is just not focused on cutting Widgets. Yesterday his machine setting was off about four hundredths of an inch. How did we find that out?

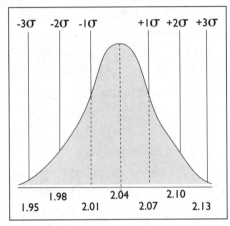

For the sake of argument, let's assume that Scott's average yesterday was 2.04 inches. In his lot, the pattern was the same as in any good lot, except the bell-shaped curve was centered over 2.04 inches, not over 2.00 inches. The standard deviation (σ) was still the same, 0.03 inches. The three-σ limits of Scott's distribution were now changed to 1.95 inches and 2.13 inches, still within the customer's specification of plus and minus 0.15 inches. Even though the customer might not complain about the higher average, he or she would probably notice it.

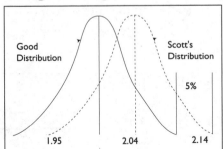

You have already seen that a good lot should vary between 1.91 inches and 2.09 inches. Five percent of the Widgets Scott was making were over the 2.09-inch limit. (You can use a statistical table to figure that out if you want to.)

If you were to pick up Widgets from Scott's machine, you would stand only 5 chances in 100, or 1 chance in 20, of getting one of the oversized pieces. Even if you were lucky enough to find one, we're sure (knowing how Scott argues with his mother-in-law) he would claim that it was just one of those freaks that really happen sometimes.

When you showed Scott his control chart, he realized his mistake and changed his machine settings. What? You do not know what a control chart is? Come on back to the army!

As you remember from way back on page 41, we were willing to give you odds of 740 to 1 that the next soldier to pass by would not be taller than 75.5 inches. We were just betting that he would not exceed the 3σ limit.

Let's change our bet to the average height of the next two soldiers. Have you ever noticed that an unusually tall soldier generally has a buddy who is on the short side? It is a safe bet that the average of the two will be nearer to the grand average of 67.7 inches than to the extreme height of 75.5 inches.

For the same odds of 740 to 1, we would have to use narrow 3σ limits. If we bet on the average of the next four soldiers, we would have to use still narrower limits. These limits are not reduced in proportion to the number of soldiers. Limits for the average of two soldiers would be about two-thirds of the limits for an individual. For the average of four soldiers, the limits would be one-half the limits for an individual. For the average of nine soldiers, the limits would be about one-third the limit for individuals.

How did we get those figures? It's elementary! Not only do measurements of individuals vary in the bell-shaped pattern of the normal curve, but sample averages vary in the same pattern. They vary around the same center. However, the standard deviation or σ of sample averages is the σ of the individuals divided by the square root of the sample size.

In the case of our soldiers, the σ of individual heights is 2.6 inches. For each sample size, we divide 2.6 inches by the square root of the sample size. You can use your calculator or computer to derive the square root. To save time, we will do the math for you.

				Three-Sigma Limits	
Soldiers' Heights					
Sample Size	Square Root of Sample Size	2.6 Divided by Square Root	3 Times Sigma of Averages	Shortest (67.7−3σ)	Tallest (67.7 +3σ)
2	2.414	2.84	5.52	62.18	73.22
4	2.000	1.30	3.90	63.80	71.60
5	2.236	1.16	3.48	64.22	71.18
10	3.162	0.82	2.46	65.24	70.16

Now, let's apply this principle to measure the Widgets from Scott Jones's machine. Assume that you take a sample of five Widgets from his machine every 15 minutes and measure them very carefully.

The standard deviation (σ) of this measurement is 0.03 inches. Dividing this by the square root of five (2.236), we get a standard deviation of 0.0134 inches for the average of five Widgets. Three σ would be 0.0402 inches.

If Scott's machine is set right, the average of five samples should vary no more than 0.04 inches above and below this center, or between 1.96 inches and 2.04 inches. As long as your sample averages vary between these limits, you can be reasonably sure that the actual average of the machine is close to the specified average of 2.00 inches. It is a 740 to 1 bet that no sample average will be higher than 2.04 inches. However, if Scott's machine setting is 2.04 inches, averages of samples of five will vary by 0.04 inches either side of this higher center. There is now a 50-50 chance that any sample average will be above 2.04 inches, instead of the 1 chance in 20 that an individual Widget will be longer than 2.09 inches. Of course, there is the same 50-50 chance that the sample average will be below 2.04 inches. However, with these odds in your favor, you are practically certain to get a high average in the first two or three samples. That is exactly what happened with Scott's machine.

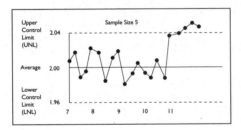

The control chart gives you a picture of all we have been saying in the last few pages. It provides an easy-to-understand graphical image of what is happening in any process. This control chart shows what happened to Scott's process.

The center line says that the Widgets should average 2.00 inches. The upper and lower dotted lines say whether the natural limits are met. They show that averages of samples of five should not be less than 1.96 inches nor more than 2.04 inches.

From 7:00 until 11:00 in the morning, Scott's sample averages zigzagged between the limits in a pattern that you expect to see in a process that is in control. Just before 11:00, the cutting tool broke and Scott put in a new one. Scott was thinking about the comeback he should have made in last night's argument with his mother-in-law. He forgot to check the setting or the new cutting tool carefully. The new setting was actually at 2.04 inches.

At 11:00, Kim O'Hollihan, the quality inspector, measured five Widgets from Scott's machine. The average looked pretty high, but it was inside the upper control limit, so Kim plotted it on the chart and let it pass. At 11:15, she took another sample. It was also inside the upper limit. However, Kim knew that the odds of two samples being so close to the upper limit were really slim. So she did not wait another 15 minutes. She took another sample right away. That sample was over the UCL. Just to be sure, she took one more. That sample was also over the 2.04 limit.

Even Scott could not argue against the evidence of the four samples, particularly the last two. He shut down the machine and checked his adjustment. He found where he had made the adjustment error. Kim stuck around and took some more samples to be sure the machine was okay and then went back to the regular 15-minute sampling intervals. Catching this adjustment error early allowed Kim and Scott to inspect only a small number of Widgets to sort out those that needed to be reworked. If the control chart had not been used, at least four hours of production from Scott's machine would have had to be examined.

Step-by-Step Directions for Making an x Bar ($\bar{x}$) and R Chart

Always make the R chart before the $\bar{x}$ chart. To complete both, follow these simple instructions.

R Chart

Step 1. Decide on the sample size (n) to be used. Typically, the sample size (n) is four or five.

Step 2. Obtain a series of groups of measurements. Each group must contain n measurements. You must have at least 10 groups of measurements; if possible, have 20 or more groups. More groups will give you better results.

Step 3. Compute the range (R) for each sample. Take the average of the R's ($\bar{R}$). $\bar{R}$ is the center line for the R chart. It is drawn as a solid horizontal line. $\bar{R}$ = average of R's of your sample groups.

Step 4. Multiply R by D_4 from the table on page 151. This gives you the upper control limit (UCL) for your control chart. The UCL is 3σ above the center line (R). Multiply R by D_3 from the table. This gives you the lower control limit (LCL) for your control chart. The LCL is 3σ below the center line ($\bar{R}$). The UCL and LCL are drawn as dotted horizontal lines.

$$UCL_R = D_4\bar{R}$$
$$LCL_R = D_3\bar{R}$$

Step 5. Use a standard control chart form and set up an appropriate scale. Control charts are usually completed on special forms. Be careful not to make the R chart too wide. Set up the R chart at the bottom of the sheet.

Step 6. Plot on this chart the successive values of R, and connect the points with straight lines.

$\bar{x}$ Chart

Step 1. Use exactly the same groups of measurements that were used for the R chart.

Step 2. Calculate the average ($\bar{x}$) for each sample. Take the average of the $\bar{x}$'s. This average of $\bar{x}$s is $\bar{\bar{x}}$; $\bar{\bar{x}}$ is the center line for the $\bar{x}$ chart. It is drawn as a solid horizontal line.

$$\bar{\bar{x}} = \Sigma\,\bar{x} \text{ divided by the number of samples.}$$

$$\Sigma = \text{"the sum of"}$$

Step 3. Multiply $\bar{R}$ by A_2 (from the table on page 151). The result is the width of the control limits for the chart. Add the $A_2\bar{R}$ value to $\bar{\bar{x}}$ to get the location of the UCL for the $\bar{x}$ chart. Subtract $A_2\bar{R}$ from $\bar{\bar{x}}$ to get the location of the LCL for the $\bar{x}$ chart. The UCL and LCL are drawn as dotted horizontal lines.

$$UCL_{\bar{x}} = \bar{\bar{x}} + A_2\bar{R}$$
$$LCL_{\bar{x}} = \bar{\bar{x}} - A_2\bar{R}$$

Step 4. Choose a scale for the $\bar{x}$ chart that is properly related to the scale that you chose for the R chart. Leave some space on the chart both above and below the limits in case any of your data samples are out of tolerance.

Step 5. Plot on this chart the successive values of $\bar{x}$, and connect the points with straight lines.

Step 6. Do something with the data. Do not ignore it. Interpret the results and take action if required.

Worksheet

Decide on the sample size (n) to be used. Typically, n is four or five. Obtain a series of groups of measurements. Each group must contain n measurements. You must have at least 10 groups of measurements. If possible, have 20 or more groups. Having more groups will give you better results. The eight-step worksheet provides a summary of the calculations for setting up a control chart.

Control Chart Summary Worksheet

Step 1: Find R = range = H – L for each subgroup.

Step 2: Find $\overline{X}$ = mean = $\dfrac{\Sigma X}{n}$ for each subgroup.

Step 3: $\overline{\overline{R}}$ = mean of ranges = $\dfrac{\Sigma R}{k}$ = _____.

Step 4: $\overline{\overline{X}}$ = mean of means = $\dfrac{\Sigma \overline{X}}{n}$ = _____.

Step 5: In the table (p. 51) look up the following values:

$$A_2 \quad = \text{\_\_\_\_\_}$$

$$D_4 \quad = \text{\_\_\_\_\_}$$

$$D_3 \quad = \text{\_\_\_\_\_}$$

Step 6: Calculate:

$$UCL_{\overline{X}} = \overline{\overline{X}} + A_2\,(\overline{R}) = \text{\_\_\_\_\_}$$

$$LCL_{\overline{X}} = \overline{\overline{X}} - A_2\,(\overline{R}) = \text{\_\_\_\_\_}$$

Step 7: Calculate:

$$UCL_R = D_4\,(\overline{R}) = \text{\_\_\_\_\_}$$

$$LCL_R = D_3\,(\overline{R}) = \text{\_\_\_\_\_}$$

Step 8: Interpret the Control Chart.

(n = subgroup size)   (k = number of subgroups)

Control Chart Concepts

The 7–7–1 Rule

7–7–l Rule

Significant Change 1—Run
Seven data points in a row on one side of the average need to be investigated.

Significant Change 2—Trend
Seven data points in a row going steadily up or down need to be investigated.

Significant Change 3—Spike
One data point outside the UCL or LCL needs to be investigated.

Control Chart Values Table

	2	3	4	5	6	7	8	9	10
D_4	3.27	2.57	2.28	2.11	2.00	1.92	1.86	1.82	1.78
D_3	0.00	0.00	0.00	0.00	0.00	0.08	0.14	0.18	0.22
A_2	1.88	1.02	0.73	0.58	0.48	0.42	0.37	0.34	0.31
d_2	1.13	1.69	2.06	2.33	2.53	2.70	2.85	2.97	3.08

Control Chart Terms

N   the number of observations in a sample; sample size.

R   range—the difference between the largest and the smallest in a given sample.

$\bar{R}$ R bar—the average of the ranges of the individual samples. A bar means total the numbers and divide by the number of numbers (average).

UCL	upper control limit. The UCL is 3σ above the center line or R bar. The upper natural limit is the point beyond which you don't normally see data.
LCL	lower control limit. The LCL is 3σ below the center line.
$\overline{X}$	average or middle.
$\overline{\overline{X}}$	the average of the X bars in your sample.
Σ	"the sum of."

Process Capability Matrix Sample

The following Cpk's are for three months of production of five different product grades with three key process characteristics

Characteristic Product	X	Y	Z
A	.7	.6	.4
B	1.4	1.2	.9
C	.8	.2	.3
D	.9	.7	.4
E	1.1	.9	.6

1. Which product best conforms to customer requirements?
2. Which product least conforms to customer requirements?
3. Which characteristic is the least capable?

The answers are in Appendix B if you need to look.

Answers to "Just for Fun"

Chapter 1

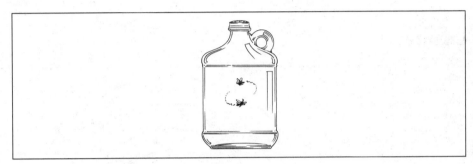

The jug will be half full in 29 minutes.
There will be 2,147,843,648 bugs in the jar after 30 minutes.

Chapter 2

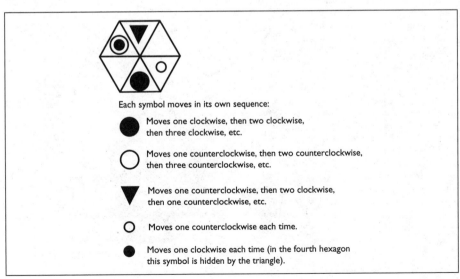

Each symbol moves in its own sequence:

⚫ Moves one clockwise, then two clockwise, then three clockwise, etc.

◯ Moves one counterclockwise, then two counterclockwise, then three counterclockwise, etc.

▼ Moves one counterclockwise, then two clockwise, then one counterclockwise, etc.

○ Moves one counterclockwise each time.

● Moves one clockwise each time (in the fourth hexagon this symbol is hidden by the triangle).

Chapter 3

You have a 33.3-percent chance of finding the treasure with your first selection. You have a 33.3-percent chance of finding treasure with your second selection. You are dealing with lids, not chests. There are three lids that cover treasure. The probability of a lid's being opened on a chest with both coal and treasure is 33.3 percent initially and remains 33.3 percent because coal and treasure are distributed identically over chests and lids.

Chapter 4

Chapter 5

Billy must sing for nine hours.

Chapter 6

Fill the 9-cup jar (A) with sugar.
Fill the 4-cup jar (B) from A.
Empty B.

Refill B from A.
Empty B.
Put the 1 cup left in A into B.
Fill B from A.
A has 6 cups in it!

Chapter 7

Each tree was sold for the same number of dollars as there were trees sold. If the number of trees is n, the total number of dollars received is n^2. Judy got both the first and last 10-dollar bills, so the number of 10-dollar bills has to be an odd number. Therefore, n must end in a digit the square of which contains an odd number of tens. Only two digits, 4 and 6, have such squares. Both squares end in 6, so n^2 is a number that ends in 6. Gary got six 1-dollar bills. Judy still owes Gary $2.00.

Chapter 8

They have played nine games.
Dan has won three.
Carolyn has won six.

Chapter 9

Chapter 10

Nancy, Joann, & Jenette play badminton, baseball, and basketball. Paul does not play any games.

Appendix A

Characteristic Product	X	Y	Z
A	.7	.6	.4
B	1.4	1.2	.9
C	.8	.2	.3
D	.9	.7	.4
E	1.1	.9	.6

Product B best performs to customer requirements.
Product C least conforms to customer requirements.
Characteristic Z is least capable.

Bibliography

Argyris, Chris, *Overcoming Organizational Defenses.* Newton, MA: Allyn & Bacon, 1990.

Burr, I. W., *Statistical Quality Control Methods.* New York: Marcel Dekker, 1976.

Deming, W. E., *Out of the Crisis.* Cambridge, MA: MIT Center for Advanced Engineering Study, 1986.

Ernst and Young, *Advanced SPC.* 1989

Ernst and Young, *Introduction to SPC.* 1989.

Harrington, H. James, *Business Process Improvement.* New York: McGraw-Hill, 1991.

Hoffherr, Glen D., et al., *Growing Teams: A Down-to-Earth Approach.* Methuen, MA: GOAL/QPC, 1993.

Hoffherr, Glen D., et al., *Making Daily Management Work: A Perspective for Leaders and Managers.* Methuen, MA: GOAL/QPC, 1992.

Hoffherr, Glen D., *The Toolbook: Decision Making and Planning for Optimum Results.* Salem, NH: Markon, Inc., 1993.

Imai, Masaaki, *Kaizen.* New York: McGraw-Hill, 1986.

Ishikawa, K., *Guide to Quality Control,* 2nd ed. Tokyo: Asian Productivity Organization, 1982.

Moen, R. D., et al., *Improving Quality through Planned Experimentation.* New York: McGraw-Hill, 1991.

Montgomery, D. C., *Introduction to Statistical Quality Control.* New York: John Wiley & Sons, 1985.

Moran, John W., et al., *A Guide to Graphical Problem-Solving Processes.* Milwaukee: ASQC Quality Press, 1990.

Orr, Ellis R., *Process Quality Control: Trouble-Shooting and Interpretation of Data.* New York: McGraw-Hill, 1975.

Reid, Robert, and Howard Scott, *Change from Within: People Make the Difference.* Washington, DC: CEEP Press, 1995.

Shewhart, W. A., *Economic Control of Quality Manufactured Product.* New York: D. Van Nostrand Company, 1931, reprinted by ASQC.

Taguchi, G., *Introduction to Quality Engineering: Designing Quality into Products and Processes.* White Plains, NY: Kraus International Publications, 1986.

Wadsworth, H. K., et al., *Modern Methods for Quality Control and Improvement* New York: John Wiley & Sons, 1986.

Western Electric Company, *Statistical Quality Control Handbook,* 2nd ed. New York: Western Electric Company, 1958.

Glossary

Assignable cause.   This is something that contributes to the variations in your process and that can be identified and tracked.

Attribute data.   These are things that are only counted, not measured (e.g., happy customers).

Check sheet.   This is a tally or record of observations. It can be used for various purposes such as gathering data for later analysis, finding out how often something is happening, finding out what kind of problems are arising, and verifying that something you believe is occurring is actually occurring. The observations you take should be as random as possible. The check sheet is a good starting point for solving most problems.

Common cause.   This is the random variation that is present within every processor system.

Common cause variations.   These are the results for variables that have been introduced into the system.

Control chart.   This is a tool that provides a picture of the way your process is performing. It is a graphical chart with control limits and plotted values. The values are a statistical measure for a series of samples or subgroups of the output of your process. A solid line shows the mean or average of your output.

Control limits.   These provide criteria for taking action or for judging the significance of variations between samples or subgroups. Upper and lower control limits are generated statistically from samples of your output. They show an approximation of how your process is working.

Control sample.   This is a frame of reference against which future output is measured.

Customer specification limits.   These provide criteria for judging what is good or bad about what you provide your customer. The upper specification limit (USL) and lower specification limit (LSL) are generated by the end user.

Dependent variable.　This is a value that is determined by the independent variable.

Frequency distribution.　Also known as a histogram, this is a measure of how often specific values occur.

Histogram.　This is a window that lets you envision or see what is happening in a process. (A graphic presentation of a data.)

Independent variable.　This is a value that affects the dependent variable.

Key success factors.　These are the things that are critical to your success. If you achieve your key success factors, you will be successful in what you are doing. If you do not achieve them, you will not be successful.

Location.　This refers to how well the distribution is centered on a target.

Lower specification limit (LSL).　The smallest value your customer will accept.

Mean.　This is the average of the numbers (data) you have collected. You find the mean by dividing the sum of all the numbers by the number of numbers you have collected. The mean (or average) also is represented by a symbol familiar to those who frequently use numbers. That statistical symbol is $\bar{x}$; it is pronounced "X bar."

Measles chart.　This is a graphical representation of the object being studied, with the data recorded on an image of the object.

Median.　This is the value of the middle item (or the average of the middle two items) when the data is arranged from the lowest to the highest number.

Mode.　This is the single number that occurs most frequently in the data you have collected.

Normal curve.　This is the bell shape that tends to be generated when any system or process is left to operate by itself.

Out-of-control process.　This is a process in which the data points fall beyond the upper or lower control limit.

Pareto principle.　This principle says that about 80 percent of the results come from about 20 percent of the causes.

Precision.　This is how uniform the spread of the numbers in your data sample are.

Process.   This is everything that works together to produce a product, a service, or other output.

Process capability (Cp).   This compares what you are currently doing with what your customer wants.

Random.   Of or designating a sample drawn from a population so that each member of the population has an equal chance to be drawn.

Range.   This is a measurement of the spread of the numbers or data you have collected. You find it by subtracting the lowest number from the highest number in your data.

Run chart.   This is a plotting of the movement of some measurement over a period of time.

Sample.   This is a small subset of what you produce. It is used to represent your entire output.

Scatter diagram.   This is a tool used to study the possible relationship between two different things that take on different values.

7–7–1 Rule   *Significant Change 1:* Seven data points in a row going steadily up or down need to be investigated. *Significant Change 2:* Seven data points in a row on one side of the average need to be investigated. *Significant Change 3:* One data point outside the UCL or LCL needs to be investigated.

Sigma or σ.   This is also known as the standard deviation.

Skewed distribution.   This occurs when the top of the normal curve is not in the middle. There is a bubble on either the left or the right side of the curve.

Special cause variations.   These occur when all planned factors are in place but something nevertheless goes wrong.

Spread.   This is the difference between the high and low values in the group of data that you are measuring.

Standard deviation.   This is a measurement of the total variability of the data. It is an average of deviations from the mean. Standard deviation also shows up very frequently as the symbol σ. This is a Greek letter used by mathematicians. It is pronounced "sigma."

Statistical control.   This refers to a process that has no assignable causes of variation. All data points fall between the upper and lower control limits.

Stratification.   This means putting like things together or separating data into subsets.

Target.   This is the exact quantity or quality that you are aiming for.

Upper and lower control limits.   These are generated statistically and show how your process is working. We don't normally see data above the upper control limit or below the lower control limit. They are the natural or normal result of the process's performance.

Variable data.   A measurement that can take on a continuous set of values (e.g., the temperature in your living room or the miles per gallon of your car.

Variation.   The extent to which things vary, one to the next. Reducing variation in inputs, methods, and output is a primary goal of Statistical Process Improvement.

Visible vector.   This is a direction that combines where you want to go with your values, mores, and competencies.

Index

ERNST & YOUNG LLP/SYSTEMCORP INC.

GUIDED TOUR

Included with this book is Ernst & Young LLP's/SystemCorp Inc.'s Multimedia Guided Tour CDROM called "Using Numbers to Make Better Decisions" and some other related information.

System Requirements:
- Windows 3.1 or higher
- Sound Blaster or comparable sound card
- CDROM Drive
- 8MB RAM
- 4MB free disk space

Installation Instructions:
1. Start Windows.
2. Load Guided Tour CD into CDROM drive.
3. Select Run from the File or Start menu.
4. Type in **<drive>:\setup** where **<drive>** is the drive letter of your CDROM drive.
5. Follow instructions given in setup program.

CONTENTS OF CDROM GUIDED TOUR

1. **Multimedia overview of this book**

2. **Authors' biographies**

3. **Other books in the series**

4. **High Tech Enablers Examples**
   To compete, today's organizations need to make effective use of technologies. Included are examples that we find helpful.
   - **ISO 9000 STEP-BY-STEP**
     An interactive multimedia application designed to help small, medium or large companies attain ISO 9000 registration much faster and at an affordable cost.
   - **PMI's Managing Projects**
     An interactive multimedia application, based on PMI's latest version of A Guide to

the PMBOK, that allows you to customize your organization's project management methodology and maximizes your ability to standardize, communicate, and control all aspects of your project through groupware task management.
   - **QS-9000 STEP-BY-STEP**
     Automotive quality system version of ISO 9000.
   - **TRACK & FLOW 9000**
     Open task management software to automate your ISO/QS-9000 documentation. Integrate existing electronic documents or design powerful forms processing capabilities in full compleance with ISO or QS.

ANY QUESTIONS?

If you need any technical assistance or more detailed product information on any of the programs demonstrated, contact **SystemCorp** at 514-339-1067.
Fax in a copy of this page to get a 10% discount on any of our products.